Sukhyang's Tale
&
Sugyŏng's Tale

Two Romantic Novels from Old Korea

Sukhyang's Tale & Sugyŏng's Tale

Two Romantic Novels from Old Korea

Texts by Anonymous Authors

Translated by

Sohn Tae-soo
Won-Chung Kim
Christopher Merrill

Homa & Sekey Books
Paramus, New Jersey

FIRST EDITION

Copyright © 2023 by Homa & Sekey Books
English translation copyright © 2023 by Sohn Tae-soo, Won-Chung Kim, and Christopher Merrill
Cover art: Chae Jongki

All rights reserved. No part of this book may be reproduced, stored in a retrieval system, or transmitted in any form, or by any means, electronic, mechanical, photocopying, recording or otherwise, without prior permission from the publisher.

Library of Congress Cataloging-in-Publication Data

Sukhyang's tale & Sugyŏng's tale : two romantic novels from Old Korea / translated by Sohn Tae-soo, Won-Chung Kim, and Christopher Merrill
ISBN 9781622461141 (paperback)
LC classification PL984.E8 S85 2023
https://lccn.loc.gov/2023020181

Published by Homa & Sekey Books
3rd Floor, North Tower
Mack-Cali Center III
140 E. Ridgewood Ave.
Paramus, NJ 07652

Tel: 201-261-8810, 800-870-HOMA
Fax: 201-261-8890
Email: info@homabooks.com
Website: www.homabooks.com

Printed in the USA
1 3 5 7 9 10 8 6 4 2

"This work was supported by the English Translation of 100 Korean Classics program through the Ministry of Education of the Republic of Korea and the Korean Studies Promotion Service of the Academy of Korean Studies (AKS-2015-KCL-1230001)."

Table of Contents

Translators' Preface   / *ix*
Introduction   / *xii*

Sukhyang's Tale   / 001
Sugyŏng's Tale   / 197

About Translators   / 249

Translators' Preface

Although translation of contemporary Korean literature into a variety of foreign languages is increasing, translation of classical Korean literature and philosophy remains sluggish. Hence the Academy of Korean Studies, which promotes research and education in Korean studies and culture, established a program to translate 100 Korean classics of literature and art, history and life, thought and religion—a timely project, interest in all things Korea having risen exponentially overseas. The need for quality translations of Korean classics is thus more acute than ever. And this translation of two famous novels from the Chosŏn dynasty (1392-1910)—*Sukhyang's Tale* (Sukhyang-chŏn) and *Sugyŏng's Tale* (Sugyŏngnangja-chŏn)—belongs to the Academy's ambitious program, partly because these stories have not appeared at home or abroad, and partly because they deal with a similar theme and background.

The novels shed light on classical Korean literature and thought, containing not only Neo-Confucian thinking—still the most important influence on Korean beliefs, ways of being, and social relations—but also elements of Taoism and Buddhism.

Sukhyang's Tale and *Sugyŏng's Tale* are noteworthy for their treatment of the essential Korean ethos. Skillfully interweaving details from real life and surrealist elements, they offer an introduction to the unique spirit of the Korean people. English-speaking readers will see how the anonymous authors elaborated a comprehensive overview of society, faith, and thought in the late Chosŏn society.

Scholars have identified 56 texts of *Sukhyang's Tale*, written in Korean or classical Chinese, which attest to its popularity. This translation is based on the Academy of Korean Studies Collection (596-R16N-001146-11), written in Korean, with supplementary materials, mostly drawn from the Ewha Womans University Collection, to fill in missing or erased parts.

For the translation of *Sugyŏng's Tale*, which is found in as many as 71 Korean-language collections, including 66 transcriptions and four printed versions, we used the 48-page Kim Dong-uk Collection as the basic text and consulted the 58-page Kim Dong-uk Collection for the missing or erased parts. This is a full translation of the source texts, with occasional bits of detail added from other versions to help readers better understand the text and the sometimes coarse, rustic, or, most importantly, omitted text from the original version.

Sukhyang's Tale and *Sugyŏng's Tale* were written as folk tales for the general public, and so we have added footnotes and subtitles to make the story line clearer. Korean names and terms have been

Romanized, and proper nouns or indigenous words, including names and places, have been spelled according to the McCune-Reischauer system, which was adopted by the Ministry of Education in the Republic of Korea and currently widely understood in the academic world both at home and abroad.

Sukhyang's Tale presented another set of problems: how to translate character and place names, since the novel was set during the Song dynasty in old China. For Chinese terms and names we adopted the Korean system instead of the Hanyu Pinyin Romanization (simplified Chinese: 汉语拼音)—the official Romanization system for Standard Chinese in mainland China—in order to avoid confusion and to emphasize the fact that *Sukhyang's Tale* is a Korean novel. We freely adopted the Chinese Hanyu Pinyin Romanization for the footnotes in *Sukhyang's Tale* to explain the names of the historical figures, places, and others when the original phonetic notation was required.

Seoul, Republic of Korea
March 2023

Introduction

Sukhyang and Sugyŏng's Tales: Where Real Life Blends with the Surreal

Korean narrative fiction, stylistically more complex than folk tales, likely emerged in the 10th century, but not until the late Chosŏn dynasty did it find favor with the general public. The lion's share of this rich tradition is divided between texts written in classical Chinese and Korean characters. Chinese was the official language, and with the invention of the Korean alphabet, or *hangŭl*, during the reign of King Sejong in the 15th century, Koreans began to use *hangŭl* in their daily lives and write novels and poems in their own language, which in due course became more popular than works composed in Chinese.

Korean academics have identified more than 1,000 fragments of classical novels, many of which exist in different transcriptions; the actual number is much larger. Only a few authors are known, the majority of the novels having been written anonymously. Scholars calculate the dates of composition by examining related works and materials; in general, authorial anonymity is a function of the fact that novels were not viewed as works of genuine literature, history, or philosophy, because they were rooted not in empirical evidence but imaginative storytelling; moreover, their popularity with women and the middle and lower classes led elites to dismiss them, believing that novels hampered efforts to promote morality; hence they played a pivotal role in describing the hopes and fears of the underprivileged.

A trend emerged among these writers to set their novels in China. Koreans shared a basic knowledge of China as a Sinocentric political paradigm; hence Korean novelists felt free to set stories in particular regions and periods of old China for works like *Sukhyang's Tale*, not as a form of flattery toward China but to re-enact real life more efficiently.

Classical Korean novels are often didactic in theme, rewarding virtue and punishing vice. Some argue that in their drive to offer lessons novelists could not accurately portray real life. Promoting virtue and reproving vice, however, proved to be an effective way to represent the people's ardent wish to rectify their harsh reality—and to find justice.

Women loved these novels. We know this because aristocrats lamented in writing that women wasted time and money reading novels. Documents suggest there were female writers, who in this strictly patriarchal society sought consolation in stories that expressed their joy and sorrow, enabled them to acquire knowledge, and refined their sensibility.

Sukhyang's Tale and *Sugyŏng's Tale*, which were quite popular in their day, feature female protagonists whose torments in an oppressive patriarchy are depicted in fantastical terms. The general public accepted a dualistic world view—readers understood the interrelatedness of the mundane and heavenly worlds—and these novels formalized varieties of imaginative hopes and dreams that could not be expressed in realistic terms.

The subject of both novels is predestined love between heavenly and earthly characters—Sukhyang and Yi Sŏn, Sugyŏng and Paek Sŏn'gun—who must overcome many obstacles to be together, which must have satisfied readers. *Sukhyang's Tale* was likely written in the 17th century, *Sugyŏng's Tale* appeared in the late 18th or early 19th century, and each reflects different sociocultural features, classical novels having emerged as a popular literary genre in the 17th century, which gave way to modern novels in the 19th century.

Sukhyang's Tale

Sukhyang's Tale is the love story of Sukhyang and Yi Sŏn, which takes place in heaven and on earth. The dozens of surviving transcriptions in vernacular Korean and classical Chinese and Japanese suggest that it enjoyed great popularity. It was used as a textbook for learning Korean and was frequently cited in other novels and poems. Thus it is no exaggeration to say that *Sukhyang's Tale* is a representative Korean novel.

It recounts Sukhyang's ordeals after being separated from her parents during a bandit riot; her reunion with Yi Sŏn, an encounter with him and then their separation; her reunion with her parents, marriage to Yi Sŏn, and his journey to the celestial world. Whenever she faces danger, a celestial figure like Grandma Magu the Fairy comes to her rescue, adding a fantastical element to the story. This dualistic world-view, in which the real and the surreal coexist, is portrayed through the close bond between the lovers in heaven and on earth, as well as in the itinerary of Yi Sŏn's journey to the celestial world.

Note that in the pre-modern period there was a widespread belief, in both the East and West, that the supernatural intervened in and influenced the mundane world. Readers of novels in the Chosŏn dynasty believed that certain celestial powers or principles would rid secular society of its absurdities and lead them to eternal blessing, regardless of religion. Even though Chosŏn society was firmly grounded in Neo-Confucian ideology, the general public believed in abstract, universal, and supernatural powers separate from any doctrine of Confucianism, Buddhism, and Daoism, all of which were amalgamated in popular culture into a view of a world where the good are rewarded and the evil are punished.

The various episodes in *Sukhyang's Tale*, in the celestial and mundane worlds, stand for real life ordeals. Although Lady Hut'o, Hermit Hwadŏk, and Grandma Magu the Fairy help her through various crises, Sukhyang, having lost her parents, wandered aimlessly, and lost everything in a fire, represents war orphans who have no place to go and no one to rely on. Her expulsion from Prime Minister Chang's house and her ill treatment by Yi Sŏn's parents reflect the suffering of ordinary people in that time. Her trials were predestined because of a misdemeanor she committed in heaven, but the novel reflects a common prejudice against war orphans—in this case one who cannot even remember her parents.

In the mid-Chosŏn dynasty, a series of wars, notably the Hideyoshi Invasion in 1592 and the Manchu Invasion in 1636, reduced the nation to chaos. The psychological scars on the national psyche found expression in novels like *Sukhyang's Tale*, which explore the ways in which that society privileged aristocrats and discriminated against the low-born. Sukhyang's ordeals thus reveal the deep-rooted gender discrimination of this patriarchal system.

The plot revolves around Sukhyang's hardships and Yi Sŏn's adventures. They have been exiled to the mundane world thanks to their love affair in heaven, but they are reunited via different routes. While Sukhyang suffers a series of hardships, Yi Sŏn is born with a silver spoon in his mouth and has an easy life until he meets her. Sukhyang has to overcome the opposition of her lover's parents, while Yi Sŏn only has to devote himself to studying for the civil service examination. Sukhyang's story has a typical ending, with her marrying her lover and reuniting with her parents, while the emperor rewards Yi Sŏn for his journey to the other world by ordering him to marry another woman of his destiny.

Women are portrayed here as passively enduring ordeals while men accomplish anything they want—a discriminative narrative that reflects the gender bias of the patriarchy. This stands in contrast to other novels of the time, which take a comparatively liberal view of gender. Although women were the main readers of novels in the 17th century, and women's narratives were becoming popular, the authorities nevertheless tried to control women, under the pretext of offering them a lesson through novels like *Sukhyang's Tale*.

Sugyŏng's Tale

Sugyŏng's Tale has been regarded as a romance novel with features similar to *Sukhyang's Tale*, since the main characters were exiled from heaven for love affairs and share fantastic adventures on the way to their reunion. While *Sukhyang's Tale* deals extensively with war, marital conflicts, and a journey to the other world, *Sugyŏng's Tale* has a simpler plot, which focuses on the close ties between Sugyŏng and Paek Sŏn'gun and a family feud. *Sugyŏng's Tale* is much shorter than *Sukhyang's Tale*.

The two stories conclude in markedly different ways. *Sugyŏng's Tale* has a happy ending. *Sugyŏng's Tale* ends in death. In *Sugyŏng's Tale*, the two main characters, exiled for flirting with each other in heaven, marry on earth—a typical story of a hermit coming down to the world as punishment. But it does not follow a typical plot. Paek Sŏn'gun returns to his house to meet his wife on his way to the state civil service examination, which leads his father to suspect her of infidelity, which leads her to kill herself, departing from traditional classical Korean narratives, where the protagonists overcome ordeals, enjoy wealth and honor, have offspring, and grow old together. Sugyŏng is reborn and ascends to heaven with Sŏn'gun, securing their eternal ties, but this is not the story of lovers pursuing happiness on earth. (One transcription even ends with a funeral service.) The novel explores the difficulty of finding true love and how a woman, left at a disadvantage, faces more severe ordeals.

Some episodes show the protagonists' ardent love: falling ill, Sŏn'gun cannot forget seeing Sugyŏng in a dream; Sugyŏng breaks the taboo, leaving Ogyŏndong to follow Sŏn'gun; Sŏn'gun gives up worldly honor and wealth to live happily with Sugyŏng. No wonder the novel is often viewed as a romance. Because it centers on the actual obstacles faced by a star-crossed couple and the tragic accidents that ensue, it is not so much a romance as a narrative of resistance to the socio-cultural fetters that hamper true love. It emphasizes the absurdities of life: the lover's dream of fulfilling love is finally unfulfilled.

This detailed portrait of the barriers to love lays bare the absurdities of a medieval Chosŏn society defined by gender discrimination and Neo-Confucian ethics. It also poses questions about the custom of matchmaking between parents of the same social status. It reveals how closed social structures infringe upon individual rights, enforces a doctrinaire ideology, and refuses any freedom in one's most important relations with others—in love and marriage. Hence the tragic death of Sugyŏng, the fairy-turned-parentless girl exiled to the mundane world, cannot overcome societal prejudices after her wedding to Sŏn'gun.

Sugyŏng's Tale does not formalize romantic love but rather portrays the anguish of the times even if it takes the form of a fantasy. If love is the most natural of human emotions, this novel exposes how cruelly the totalitarian feudal order represses the most important relationships. Describing the failure of two lovers to make a happy life, this novel tugs at the heartstrings of any reader alert to the looming possibility of tragic love.

Lee, Jee Ha
Associate Professor of Korean literature
Sungkyunkwan University, Seoul

Sukhyang's Tale

Main Characters

- **Kim Sukhyang**: Daughter of Kim Chŏn. Because of a crime committed in heaven, she is fated to be separated from her parents at the age of five and endure five near-death experiences before turning fifteen. She marries her heaven-sent lover Yi Sŏn and becomes the Lady of High Virtue and Chastity.
- **Yi Sŏn**: Son of Duke Yi of Wi. He searches for Sukhyang upon learning that she is his heaven-sent mate. After secretly marrying her, he temporarily parts with her to acquire mysterious medicines for the dying empress dowager by the order of the Emperor.
- **Magu the Fairy**: An aide to Sukhyang, who descends to the secular world from Mount Ch'ŏnt'ae, by the order of Wŏlgung Hang'a, to save Sukhyang and then lives with her in the Yihwa Public House. She returns to the mountain after fulfilling her mission.
- **Kim Chŏn**: Father of Sukhyang. Born to Master Unsu, he parts with his daughter and reunites with her after she suffers her predestined ordeals.
- **Mrs. Kim**: The wife of Kim Chŏn, mother of Sukhyang, and daughter of Chang Hoe.
- **Duke Yi of Wi**: Father of Yi Sŏn. After learning that his son has secretly married Sukhyang, he tries to kill her so that his son can marry Maehyang, daughter of the King of Yang. When he learns that Sukhyang is his heaven-sent daughter-in-law, he comes to respect her. His full name is Yi Chŏng.

- **Lady Yi:** The wife of Duke Yi of Wi. She bears Yi Sŏn after praying for a baby at the Taesŏng Temple.
- **Lady Yŏ:** The eldest sister of Duke Yi of Wi. She orchestrates Yi Sŏn's wedding with Sukhyang.
- **Prime Minister Chang:** He raises Sukhyang as his adopted daughter for five years after she has parted from her parents. He banishes her at his maid servant Sahyang's false charges of her. He meets her again after she becomes the Lady of High Virtue and Chastity. His full name is Chang Song.
- **Lady Chang:** Prime Minister Chang's wife. Her maid servant Sahyang's slander prompts her to tell her husband that Sukhyang stole her jewels. She later regrets this.
- **Sahyang:** A maid servant in Prime Minister Chang's house, who viewed Sukhyang as her rival. Nursing a grudge, she accuses her of stealing from Prime Minister and Lady Chang and is put to death by heaven.
- **Hermit Hwadŏk:** The god of fire. He rescues Sukhyang from being burned to death in a grass fire on a field of eulalia.
- **Lady Hut'o:** The goddess of land. She invites Sukhyang to the underworld and guides her to the house of Prime Minister Chang.
- **The Emperor:** The sovereign monarch who respects the loyalty of Duke Yi of Wi and his son, Yi Sŏn. When the death of the empress dowager is imminent, he orders Yi Sŏn to go on a journey to acquire medicines for her.

- **Maehyang:** Princess of the King of Yang. Her pen name is Sŏljungmae. After the King of Yang's proposal to marry her into the Duke of Yi's family is annulled, she insists on marrying Yi Sŏn, tied to him from her previous life.
- **Dragon King:** He repays his gratitude to Kim Chŏn for saving his daughter from being killed, first with a pair of mysterious jade beads and then by ordering his prince to help Yi Sŏn on his journey to acquire medicines.
- **Prince of Dragon King:** Son of the Dragon King. He accompanies Yi Sŏn and assists him during their journey through twelve countries.

The list of the names and the explanations in "Main Characters" are not part of the original text but have been added by translators in order to help readers understand the story better.

Sukhyang's Birth

Once there was a man named Kim Chŏn [1], a premier's son, who lived in Namyang [2] in the Song dynasty [3] in old China. Born into a distinguished family and blessed with extraordinary talent, Kim surpassed Han T'oe-chi [4] and Yi Chŏk-sŏn [5] in writing and Cho Maengpu [6] and Wang Hŭiji [7] in calligraphy. Renowned scholars from across the country flocked to his house.

---

[1] Because this novel was written in Korean during the late Chosŏn dynasty, this translation basically adopts the Romanization of the Korean alphabet for proper nouns, including the names of protagonists, titles and places, notwithstanding the fact that the story is set in the Song dynasty (960-1279) in old China. This translation basically follows the McCune-Reischauer system of Korean Romanization.

[2] Namyang, or Nanyang (南陽) in Chinese, is a town in the Yangyang Prefecture of Hubei Province in China.

[3] The Song dynasty lasted from 960 until 1279.

[4] Han T'oe-chi, or Han Yu (韓愈; 768-824) in Chinese, was a noted Tang dynasty essayist and poet.

[5] Yi Chŏk-son, aka Li Zhexian (李謫仙; 701-762)) or Li Bai (李白) in Chinese, was an acclaimed Tang dynasty poet.

[6] Cho Maeng-pu, or Zhao Mengfu (趙孟頫; 1254-1322) in Chinese, was an esteemed Chinese painter and calligrapher in the Yuan dynasty.

[7] Wang Hŭiji, or Wang Xizhi (王羲之; 303-361) in Chinese, was a noted Chinese calligrapher in the Jin dynasty.

His father, Master Unsu, was a man unparalleled across the nation in terms of noble virtue and talent. In recognition of his honors, the Emperor offered him the posts of royal advisor and minister of personnel affairs. Adamantly having opposed to accepting these posts, Master Unsu went into seclusion in the forest and after nine years starved to death. Overcome with grief, Kim buried his father in the family tomb with the proper rituals and mourned his dead spirit for three years[8], leaving his family destitute.

One day Kim was on his way to visit a close friend to congratulate him on securing the governor-generalship of a prosperous district. Crossing the Pan River[9] with a donkey loaded with wine in gourd-shape bottles and a sumptuous meal, he saw some fishermen on the riverside about to grill a large turtle they had just caught. On closer inspection, he saw that the sad turtle was crying, with tears flowing from its eyes. Struck with strange thoughts, Kim came closer to the animal and found the Chinese character *chŏn* (天)[10] inscribed on its forehead and two other

---

[8] Chinese and Koreans traditionally observed three years of mourning for their deceased parents, according to Confucian proprieties.

[9] Pan River is known as Panheshui (盤何水) in Chinese and Banhe (半何) in other versions of the text. "He (何)" and "shui (水)" refer to a river and water, respectively, in Chinese.

[10] *Chŏn*, or *Tian* in Chinese means "heaven."

characters—*su* (壽) [11] and *pok* (福) [12] —clearly emblazoned on its abdomen. Thinking it must be an auspicious animal, Kim said to the fishermen, "Please don't kill the turtle. Won't you release it back into the water?"

The fishermen replied, "We cast nets all day long without catching anything except this turtle. It is an auspicious animal, but we'll cook it to stave off our hunger."

Feeling compassion, Kim opened his knapsack and offered his traveling expenses of fifteen coins, bottles of wine, and his meal in exchange for the ill-fated turtle, which he released into the water. It kept looking back at him until it disappeared.

A year passed. One day Kim was crossing the Paegun Bridge on his way home from meeting a friend. When he approached the middle of the bridge, the raging waters swamped both ends of the bridge. Helpless, Kim had no choice but to grasp a pillar of the collapsing bridge. After a while, he saw a certain figure shaped like a black plank drifting toward him. In desperation, he abandoned the pillar and jumped onto it. The figure flinched and swam with four legs as fast as a flying arrow. It crossed the river and set Kim down on a rock on the other bank. Then it hid its body under the water and poked its head up. Kim watched the creature, with the character *ch'ŏn* (天) distinct on its forehead. Taken

---

[11] *Su*, or *Shou* in Chinese means "longevity."
[12] *Pu*, or *Fu* in Chinese means "good fortune."

aback, Kim thought, "The turtle I rescued in the Pan River must have repaid my favor." Many times he bowed to it in gratitude.

After a while, the turtle spewed a mist that formed a mysterious rainbow around him. As the hazy energy lifted, Kim saw two beads—each the size of a swallow egg—under his feet. Taking a closer look, he saw them shining brilliantly in many colors, emitting an aroma. Two delicate Chinese letters could be seen on the beads: *su* (壽) and *pu* (福).

"The turtle has returned my favor of saving its life at the Pan River," Kim told himself. He bowed to it many times in gratitude, and then returned home.

*　*　*

At the age of twenty Kim Chŏn was very poor and unable to find a woman to marry. Meanwhile there was a man named Chang Hoe living in the town of Yŏngch'ŏn [13]. Honest and indifferent to his reputation, Chang devoted himself to farming. Though he was the well-off scion of a renowned and prosperous family, he had no sons but only a daughter, who was second to none across the land in beauty and talent. Searching for a suitable son-in-law, he heard through the grapevine that Kim Chŏn was an excellent writer and a fine man. Chang asked him to marry his daughter. For a wedding gift Kim could

---

[13] Yŏngch'ŏn, or Yingchuan (潁川) in Chinese, is a town in Henan Province.

only afford to send two beads to the bride's house.

Chang's wife looked at the beads, lamenting, "A galaxy of rich and talented men has competed to marry our daughter. Why didn't you listen to me instead of choosing such a poor man to be our son-in-law?"

Chang said, "Only barbarians prioritize property in marriage. Kim is poor for now, but someday he will surely take a high government position. How can we covet only wealth? Besides, these beads are the most precious jewels in the world."

Chang ordered a master jade craftsman to carve the beads into a pair of rings, which he gave to his daughter. He set a date for the wedding, and hosted a proper ceremony. The newlyweds loved each other so much that they resembled a pair of mandarin ducks enjoying the blue water or thrushes dwelling on the fused boughs of two separate trees[14].

Ten years after the wedding, Chang and his wife passed away. Kim buried them in the family gravesite with the proper devotions, and took over the household affairs. Although no one could equal the Kims in terms of wealth and honor, they still had no child. So they journeyed into the auspicious mountains and prayed with all their heart and soul for a child. On the fifteenth of July, in the Year of Muja[15], Kim and his wife went up to the Wanwŏl

---

[14] "A pair of mandarin ducks" and "the fused boughs of two separate trees" are metaphors for the most devoted married couples in Korea.

[15] The Year of Muja (戊子) is the 25th year in the Chinese

Pavilion to behold the beauty of the moon. A white flower blossom suddenly fell at the feet of Mrs. Kim[16]. Surprised, she noticed that the flower, which was neither a pear blossom nor a Japanese apricot, gave off an intense fragrance. Then a strong gust tore it to pieces. Bewildered, Mrs. Kim heaved a deep sigh.

She dreamed that night of a golden toad entering her breast. Waking astonished, she told her husband. He said, "Yesterday, a cinnamon tree blossom fell at your feet and last night a golden toad entered your breast in a dream. This must be a sign that we will have a precious child." Kim happily prayed for that. As if by magic, Mrs. Kim became pregnant that month.

Time flew by, and one fine day in her tenth month of pregnancy five-colored clouds[17] suddenly circled

---

sexagenary cycle, aka Stems-and-Branches (干支)—a cycle of sixty terms used for recording days and years.

[16] Mrs. Kim was the wife of Kim Chŏn and daughter of the late Chang Hoe. In Korea, the wife does not change her surname to her husband's after marriage. This translation, however, follows the Western style to avoid confusion, partly because some of the surnames of the female characters, including Prime Minister Chang's wife, were not mentioned in the text.

[17] Five-colored clouds mean auspicious heavenly spirits, which appear in old novels of Korea and in this novel, too. In East Asia, including Korea, there were five colors—white, red, blue, yellow, and black—compared with seven in the West, thanks to the principle of five elements and yin and ying. Thus rainbows in the East had five major colors, which

the Kim's house, filling it with an unusual fragrance. While all the household members thought it strange, two fairies came down from the sky after sunset. They lit a lamp and told Kim, "Wŏlgung Hang'a[18] will come here soon. Please remove every filthy thing from the house."

When the fairies entered Mrs. Kim's boudoir, Kim, still in a daze, ordered the ladies-in-waiting to clean the house. A mysterious light shone from the house to the sky, and the fragrance spilled everywhere. Afraid that his wife might die in childbirth, Kim peeped into the room and saw that she had just delivered a baby. The fairies washed the newborn with perfume, laid it down beside its mother, and left in haste. Kim tried to chase after them, but their whereabouts were unknown: they had disappeared in a flash. Hurrying back to the room, Kim found his wife unconscious. Kim woke her and sat her up. It was as if she had awakened from sleep. The fragrance stayed in the house for three months, and

---

were related to the five directions of the world: east, west, south, north, and center. This is analogous to the five traditional Korean musical tones, Gung, Sang, Gak, Chi, Wu, compared with seven in Western music– do, re, me, fa, sol, la, ti.

[18] The text in the Ewha Womans University Collection reads, "Now your lady will come down here soon," using "your lady" instead of "Wŏlgung Hang'a (月宮姮娥)," which is more appropriate in the context, since Sukhyang was formerly Wŏlgung Soa, not Wŏlgung Hang'a. Wŏlgung Hang'a, literally Hang'a in the Moon Palace, appears several times hereafter in this text.

so Kim named his daughter Sukhyang[19] and also gave her the pen name of Wŏlgung Sŏn[20].

Sukhyang turned three, developing a royal air. Her face was so beautiful that people did not dare look at her directly. What's more, her voice was as lovely as the sound of a jade pipe, and she seemed so mature that Kim feared she might die young[21]. One day he had his daughter's fortune told by a physiognomist named Wang Kyun.

After examining Sukhyang, Wang said, "This child is not part of the mundane world. She was born with the spirit of Wŏlgung Hang'a[22], and she will become a great figure. But since she was exiled to the secular world, having committed a crime against heaven, she will see better days only after she repays her debt from her previous life. In short, she will have rough start, but will enjoy great fortune when she is older."

Kim said, "I admit that, of course, we cannot know what will become of her in later life. But since we are well-off, what misfortune could come to her?"

---

[19] Sukhyang (淑香), the title-role of this novel, means "clear fragrance."

[20] Wŏlgung Sŏn (月宮仙) means "a fairy in the Moon Palace."

[21] In East Asia, including Korea, people have long thought that beauty is often incompatible with luck, which means the fairest flowers or beautiful women fade the soonest.

[22] Wŏlgung Hang'a (月宮姮娥; literally Hang'a of the Moon Palace): Hang'a here refers to a title of the supreme celestial fairy living in the Moon Palace in ancient China.

Wang Kyun answered with a smile, "No one can predict what will happen in the future. From reading your daughter's fortune based on the "four pillars of destiny [23]," I can say that she is destined to be separated from her parents at the age of five, roam around with no specific destination, and meet the misfortune of near-death five times before she turns fifteen. She will be given the title of Lady of High Virtue and Chaste [24] at seventeen, and will be reunited with her parents at twenty, enjoying peace and prosperity thereafter. She will ascend to heaven at the age of seventy."

Kim said, "If she is destined to part from us in infancy, how will she recognize us later even if she is alive? In that case, we, too, will not recognize her." On a piece of soft silk Kim wrote down the name and other name of his daughter, and the hour, date, month, and year of her birth, put it into a small bag with a piece of Mrs. Kim's jade pair rings, and tied it to a coat string of the daughter's dress.

Misfortune Begins

---

[23] The four pillars of destiny is a traditional way of describing the four components that supposedly determine a person's fate. The "four pillars (四柱)," or the "four components," refer to the moment of birth; i.e. year, month, day, and hour. They are used alongside fortune-telling practices in Chinese and Korean astrology.

[24] In the Chosŏn dynasty, the title was bestowed by the government on a lady who maintained her fidelity and perfectly followed social proprieties and principles.

Sukhyang turned five. Bandits rose up that year and invaded Hyŏngch'o²⁵. Many people, including those in Kim Chŏn's village, abandoned their houses and took refuge. Kim took his family to Kangnŭng²⁶. They encountered bandits along the way and lost all their male servants and property. Kim narrowly escaped the deadly scene with his wife and daughter. With the bandits on their heels, Kim and his wife, exhausted, could no longer keep running and were at their wit's end.

Wailing, Kim said to his daughter, "My dear Sukhyang, hold tight to my neck." Kim ran on with his daughter hanging on. Falling face-first into the ground and tumbling over backwards, he got up and ran again until he was almost out of breath and completely exhausted.

Kim said to his daughter, "The bandits are right behind us, and I'm afraid we'll all die. You must hide under this rock. We'll come back for you tomorrow." He scooped steamed rice into a small bowl and gave it to Sukhyang. Wailing with his wife, he said, "Dear Sukhyang, eat boiled rice when you're hungry and

---

²⁵ Hyŏngch'o, or Jingchu (荊楚) in Chinese, is located in in Hyŏngju, or Jingzhou (荊州) in the land of Chu (楚) in old China.

²⁶ Kangnŭng, or Jiangling (江陵) in Chinese, was the seat of government in the Chu dynasty during the Spring and Autumn and the Warring States periods in ancient China. It is now located in Hubei Province.

drink water when you're thirsty."

Kim and his wife could not leave immediately. But watching the bandits chase after them and kill people as if they were cutting dried grass, they had no choice but to leave the young girl among the crowd of bandits.

Sukhyang caught her mother's skirt and cried, "Mama, don't leave me alone! Papa, I will follow you!" Holding her mother's skirt with one hand and clutching her father's belt with the other, Sukhyang sobbed and begged her parents to take her with them. Kim and his wife could not easily leave, and the bandits came closer—right under their nose. Terrified, Kim grasped his daughter's wrists and put her between the rocks, blocking them with a big stone so that she would not follow them. Giving her a bowl of rice, Kim soothed the crying girl, "Sukhyang, my daughter, you must stay here. We'll bring you something to eat from home."

Kim told his wife to hurry, forcing her to quicken her steps. Helplessly led away by her husband, Mrs. Kim looked back at her daughter. Sukhyang peeked out from the rocks and wept, holding the bowl of boiled rice with one hand and wiping her eyes with the other. She called her mother until her voice gradually hushed. Mrs. Kim kept weeping, turning her head toward her daughter, refusing to move forward. How pathetic it was to see the miserable faces of Mrs. Kim and the wretched little girl! It was beyond description. Mrs. Kim kept looking back, but Kim picked up his pace, running far away until Sukhyang's crying could no longer be heard. Seized with pain, as if their intestines had split and their bodies melted, the husband and wife could not even weep.

Meantime a bandit found Sukhyang and said, "Where are your parents? If you lie to me, I will chop you up with this sword."

Sukhyang cried louder yet. "My parents left me, saying, 'We'll bring you something to eat from home.' But they haven't come back, so how can I know where they are?"

When the bandit tried to kill her, one of his companions stopped him, saying, "How can you kill an innocent weeping girl abandoned by her parents. Look at her lovely face! She will become a great figure. If we leave her here, beasts will eat her."

The bandit descended the mountain, carrying Sukhyang. When he came to a remote village, he put her down and said, "I pity you, beautiful girl. I have a child as lovely as you. I know the pain of your parents who had to desert you." He tapped her on the back. "Stay here. Your parents will eventually come back for you." The bandit kept looking at her as he left.

At a loss where to go, Sukhyang paced back and forth, wailing, missing her parents. But where on earth could she find them? The refugees took compassion on Sukhyang and wept for her as they watched her weep and wander about. Evening shadows fell, night advanced, the wind raged. Sukhyang clutched her cold feet, lay down flat, and wept, calling for her mother. Then a pair of blue cranes flew down. One covered Sukhyang with its wings and put the jujubes it carried in its mouth into hers, saving her from cold and hunger.

Meantime Mrs. Kim said to her husband, "Night has fallen, and the bandits may have moved to another place. You'd better search for Sukhyang now." Kim looked for her, finding only dead bodies in the fields. No sign of Sukhyang. Not knowing what to do, he returned to Mrs. Kim, weeping, "I couldn't even figure out if she is alive or dead."

Mrs. Kim fainted, and when she came to her senses, she said, "Where will I see my daughter again? Oh, heaven! How can I live after losing my child? If you really care for the love between a mother and a daughter, please let me see her again before I die."

In excruciating pain, as if her heart was tearing apart, she prayed to the Big Dipper[27] every day. "I wish I could meet Sukhyang again." She wept, fell asleep, and in a dream saw Sukhyang enter her room, calling, "Mama." Sukhyang sat on her lap and sobbed, rubbing her cheek against her mother. Thrilled, Mrs. Kim embraced her, crying bitterly, "My dear Sukhyang, where have you been all this time?" Mrs. Kim stroked her lovingly before she woke to find it was just a dream. She said in grief, "Maybe I saw the ghost of Sukhyang. Has she died somewhere and has her spirit come to see me?" Mrs. Kim thumped the ground, shedding bloody tears from her eyes and blood from her mouth. Mountains and streams, plants and grass, all lamented for her.

Sukhyang wept, roaming aimlessly from place to

---

[27] Koreans used to pray to the Big Dipper for good luck.

place, with no one to rely on. The sound of her crying was sad enough to melt the minds and bodies of her listeners. After a while, a red bird appeared from afar, alighted on her lap, then flew away. Sukhyang followed the bird across many mountains until she saw a village, which she entered, weeping and calling for her mother. The villagers took pity on her. "Where are your parents?" they asked.

Sukhyang wept for a long time. "My mother told me she would come to pick me up the next day. But she hasn't returned." Everyone cried. Because Sukhyang was very beautiful and gracious, people wanted to raise her as their daughter. But no one dared suggest they live together, because they had to move around, taking refuge. Instead they fed and consoled her, "We're taking refuge in the mountains. You must stop weeping and find somewhere to stay."

Kim hid his wife deep in the mountains and went down to the village to search for Sukhyang again, but could not find her. He thought, "Sukhyang must have been dead." When he told Mrs. Kim this, she fainted again.

When Mrs. Kim recovered, Kim consoled her, "She couldn't have gone too far away, since she is so young. Perhaps someone is taking care of her. Please don't be sorrowful anymore. Remember what Wang Kyun predicted years ago."

Mrs. Kim replied, "How can I forget her when memories of her still glimmer in my eyes and the sound of her crying rings in my ears from the moment of our separation?" She cried again. The pitiful scene was beyond description.

***

While Sukhyang roamed about after losing contact with the villagers and the bird, she looked at a distant mountain, where some people were loitering. She followed a rugged road into the mountains, and when evening fell, she leaned on a tree, unable to endure her hunger anymore. At that moment a blue bird[28] arrived from somewhere, with a flower in its beak, and perched on the back of her hand. When she ate the flower, she reawakened with a clearer mind.

Following the blue bird, she crossed two hills. Soon afterward, a woman appeared, held Sukhyang in her arms, and put her down in front of a large hall. There a Lady in a ceremonial coronet and dresses embroidered with the seven treasures [29] sat on a golden chair. Seeing Sukhyang, the Lady came down from the chair, bowed to her, and said, "Please sit on a chair on the east side."

When Sukhyang kept weeping, unsure what to do, the Lady said, "You, a fairy, must have drunk dirty water when you came down to earth. Please drink this. It's a mysterious nectar just for hermits."

The Lady ordered her maids to pour dew tea into

---

[28] Blue (or green) birds, *qingniao* (青鳥) in Chinese, which appear in old Chinese literature, are generally regarded as messengers.

[29] The Seven Treasures are gold, silver, lapis, crystal, coral, agate, and pearl.

an agate glass on an amber tray for Sukhyang. After drinking the sweet aromatic tea, Sukhyang vividly recalled what happened to her in heaven and what hardships she had suffered when she was separated from her parents on earth. She was a child with the mind of an adult. She raised her head to express her gratitude to the Lady: "I heartily thank you for your kindness in extending hospitality to a girl who has suffered hardships in the world on account of her serious crime in heaven."

Smiling, the Lady said, "You still don't recognize me, do you?"

"I'm sorry, I don't. I'm still a little confused."

"You've come to the netherworld. I'm Lady Hut'o[30]. Because you suffered through a series of ordeals in the world, I sent you a green monkey[31], a blue crane, a red bird, and a blue bird in succession. You remember seeing them, don't you?"

"Yes, I saw them all."

When Lady Hut'o offered Sukhyang another cup of tea, she drank it all and lamented. "You brought me here and treated me cordially when I was destitute. I wish I could repay even an infinitesimal part of my gratitude by serving you as a maid."

The Lady lowered herself, fixing her makeup. "I am

---

[30] Lady Hut'o (后土夫人) is the goddess of land. "T'o (土)" means land.

[31] A green monkey is an auspicious animal, like a blue crane and a bluebird, and represents Lady Hut'o's affection. The green monkey has not been mentioned yet in this text, perhaps because of a textual error.

no more than a humble fairy in the underworld. But you are the supreme fairy of the Moon Palace, and what hardships you have suffered are momentary. Since it's already dark, why don't you spend the night here with me and leave tomorrow?"

The Lady threw a big party for Sukhyang, who had never seen in the secular world the dishes and food prepared for the feast. The Lady offered Sukhyang cup after cup of nectars, and as her mind cleared she gradually forgot about the mundane world and began to recollect what had happened to her in heaven.

Sukhyang asked the Lady, "I heard long ago that the Ten Kings of the Underworld live in the other world. Is that true?"

"Yes, it is.[32]"

"Where is the Hall of the Ten Kings[33]?" Sukhyang asked.

"Not far from here," the Lady replied.

Sukhyang said, "I lost my parents of the mundane world during a bandit riot. I'm worried that they might have passed away. If so, they'll be in the Hall of the Ten Kings. I should go meet them."

The Lady smiled. "Your parents of the mundane world are still alive. But you must know that they, too, are not ordinary people. He was a hermit officer[34]

---

[32] This paragraph is missing in the text and is borrowed from the text in the Ewha Womans University Collection.

[33] The Ten Kings (十王) are the Ten Kings of the Underworld.

[34] A hermit officer is a translation of *sŏn'gun*, or *xianguan*

and she was a fairy, respectively, on Mount Pongnae[35]. Like you, they were exiled for their crimes in heaven but are destined to return to the mountain in due course."

"When I go back to the secular world, can I see my parents again?" Sukhyang asked.

"When you were in the Moon Palace, you committed a crime against Wŏlgung Hang'a, who decided to make you suffer. When Pongsŏn[36] the fairy begged the Great Jade Emperor to save you, Hang'a grew angry, sent her to the secular world, and made her the Lady of Prime Minister Chang in Namgun[37]. Thus you must first go to Prime Minister Chang's house to express your gratitude to his wife, enjoy your glory upon meeting Hermit T'aeŭl[38], and then see your parents again. It will take ten years plus five more for you to be completely free of your predestined ordeals."

"When I think of hardships in the world, one day

(仙官) in Chinese, an immortal with a title in the celestial world.

[35] Mount Pongnae, or Mount Penglai (蓬萊山) in Chinese, is one of the legendary mountains for hermits in old China.

[36] Pongsŏn is called Kyusŏng (奎星) in the text in the Ewha Womans University Collection.

[37] Namgun, or Nanjun (南郡) in Chinese, located in the Hubei Province, was one of the seven commendaries of Hyŏngju (Jingzhou).

[38] Hermit T'aeŭl (太乙) is the supreme celestial hermit among heavenly gods.

seems to last three years. How can I endure fifteen more years? I would rather take my life," Sukhyang said.

"Whether you like it or not, you're destined to suffer through five deadly ordeals before you enjoy any happiness. First, you escaped from the ill fortune of death by the sword of bandits on Mount Panya[39]. Second, you've avoided the ill fortune of dying in the underworld. Now that you have experienced two hardships, three more are left. Therefore you must be extremely careful," the Lady said.

"What kind of crime did I commit in my previous life to lead Hang'a to punish me so severely?" Sukhyang wondered. During her conversation with Lady Hut'o, offering nectars to each other, they heard a monkey cry in a distant village.

"Though I enjoy this precious time to talk with you, you have a long way to go," said the Lady. "Now it's time for you to leave. So please get up from your seat."

"I'm a stranger in this land. Where can I find someone to trust?" Sukhyang asked.

"Don't worry. I will give you directions to your destination. You must visit the house of Prime Minister Chang first and express your gratitude to his wife."

"How far is Namgun from here?"

---

[39] Panya, or Bore (般若; Prajñā in Sanskrit) in Chinese, means wisdom in Buddhism. Mount Panya is a fictitious place.

"It's about two thousand and three hundred *li*[40] to Namgun. But don't worry about how to get there." The Lady broke a branch of a tree in a golden pot and hung it around the antlers of a white deer. "Ride this deer, and you will come to your destination in a flash, no matter how far it is. When you're hungry, eat these fruits," the Lady said.

Sukhyang bade farewell to Lady Hut'o and rode on the deer, which ran-flew through the clouds. When the deer stopped running-flying, Sukhyang climbed down off its back. Hungry, she filled her stomach with fruits hanging from the antlers. She forgot what happened in heaven. Regaining the mind of a child, she feared the deer might bite her.

Sukhyang Settles into Prime Minister Chang's Family

The bright moon sank below a western mountain, and darkness fell. Unsure of where to go, Sukhyang sat down and fell asleep: she was in Prime Minister Chang's garden.

Living in Namgun, Prime Minister Chang was heir to Chang Chabang [41] of the Han dynasty. He

---

[40] *Li*, a traditional Korean unit of distance, is approximately 0.393 kilometers. Two thousand and three hundred *li* is approximately 900 km.

[41] Chang Chabang, spelled here according to Korean Romanization, like others in this text, is Zhang Zifang (張子房), aka Zhang Liang (張良; 3rd century BC~186 BC), a government official in the Western Han dynasty.

acquired a good reputation by passing the civil service examination before he was twenty and entered government service in many posts. He was named Prime Minister before turning forty, having served three emperors, and stood second to none in wealth and acclaim, long honored as a meritorious official. When the nation entered a period of political turmoil during the reign of Emperor Sinjong [42], Prime Minister Chang gave up his government post and refused to enter the Royal Court. When bandits revolted in the frontier areas of the nation, some government ministers lodged an appeal with the Emperor, declaring that Chang had communicated secretly with the bandits. When the Emperor deprived Chang of his government post and expelled him from the capital, Chang returned to his hometown and dedicated himself to household affairs. Although his house was filled with gold and jewels, as well as servants and land, Chang always lamented having no children.

One day Lady Chang, the Prime Minister's wife, dreamed that a fairy came down from a cloud and offered her a laurel branch, saying, "Because you committed a serious crime in your last life, you are doomed to childlessness. But it's pathetic to grieve over this misfortune, so I offer you this flower. Cherish it. You will come to understand its meaning later."

---

[42] Sinjong, or Shenzong (神宗; 1048~1085) in Chinese, was the sixth emperor of the Song dynasty.

Upon waking, she told this story to her husband, who said, "Heaven must have understood that we are grieving over having no child and has decided to bless us with one. But since we are both over fifty, how can we dare expect to have a child?"

He stood up and entered a thatched cottage of the house.

Then five-colored clouds glimmered in the garden with an auspicious energy that filled the atmosphere and a mysterious fragrance spread through the garden. Chang thought, "Now it is October in winter—not a season for watching five-colored mists. Where on earth could such mysterious fragrance arise?"

With a goosefoot cane, he ascended into the garden and saw new leaves and the blossoming flowers of a peony tree, under which a little girl was dozing. Amazed, Chang studied the girl, who had a vital energy between her eyebrows and a figure mysterious enough to startle anyone. Impressed by her appearance, he immediately called a lady-in-waiting, "Go quickly and tell my wife what I saw here!"

Surprised by the voice, the girl woke up and burst into tears. He asked her several questions: "Who on earth are you? Where do you live? How old are you? What is your name? And why did you doze off in this garden?"

Shedding teardrops shaped like pearls on her jade-like cheek, Sukhyang replied, "My name is Sukhyang. I don't know where my house is. Mother left me by the rocks, saying 'I'll come back tomorrow to pick you up,' but never returned. With nowhere to go, I roamed aimlessly. Then an animal gave me a ride on its back and put me down here."

Chang thought. "She has lost her parents." He introduced Sukhyang to his wife, who thought she resembled the fairy she saw in her dream and had the same voice. She said, "She is the heaven-sent child, so we must raise her." She took Sukhyang into the house, fed and dressed her, and raised her in her arms like her own child.

Years passed. By the time Sukhyang turned seven, she was gifted in everything from understanding letters she had never been taught to embroidering, sewing, and even spinning. Because she was wiser than others, Prime Minister Chang and his wife were very happy. When Sukhyang turned ten, Lady Chang entrusted her with supervising all the household affairs. Sukhyang not only sincerely served Prime Minister Chang and his wife but also oversaw the servants, while holding heartfelt memorial services for the family ancestors. She did more than ten people combined.

One day Prime Minister and Lady Chang praised Sukhyang: "She is praiseworthy in terms of her talents, appearance, and conduct. Let's marry her into a noble family and entrust her with our future affairs." The servants deemed this a good idea.

Meantime there was a maid servant named Sahyang living in the house, who had been in charge of all the household affairs before Sukhyang arrived. Deprived of all her rights after Sukhyang's arrived, Sahyang had long nursed a grudge against her new rival and tried to kill her. Only she had not gotten a proper chance to carry out the evil scheme.

Time passed. Sukhyang turned fifteen, unparalleled in her countenance and work ethic. Lady Chang asked her husband to marry Sukhyang off to a prominent family.

* * *

One day Sukhyang escorted the Changs to a party in the Yŏngch'un Pavilion to look at the spring scenery. An evening magpie[43] flew into her, cried three times, and flew away to the east. Surprised, Sukhyang said to the Prime Minister, "A magpie symbolizes the spirit of a girl. It flew into me before it cried and flew away. It might be an ill omen."

Finding this ominous, Prime Minister Chang was deeply worried.

Sahyang, to her joy, found the house empty, the others joining a party in the back garden. She went into Lady Chang's boudoir and stole a golden phoenix hairpin—a wedding gift—and an encased ornamental jade knife bestowed by the Emperor on Prime Minister Chang. These she put in a bridal box of cosmetics in Sukhyang's room.

Three days later, Lady Chang looked in vain for

---

[43] An evening magpie is not a particular breed but literally a magpie crying in the evening. In old Korea, a magpie was an auspicious animal, unlike in Western thought, while a crow was an inauspicious animal. But people believed that a magpie crying in the evening brings bad luck, while a magpie crying in the morning brings fortune.

the golden hairpin before leaving for a village party. Embarrassed, she took out all the household goods and examined them until she noticed that the Prime Minister's jade knife was also missing. Thinking it weird, Lady Chang severely interrogated the servants.

Making the most of it, Sahyang pretended to come in from outside and hurried to the scene, as if she knew nothing. She asked her fellow servants, "Why is the house in such an uproar. Has something happened?"

The servants were so perplexed and busy that no one answered her.

"I lost two treasures and I am searching for them." Lady Chang said.

Sahyang whispered to her, "I saw Sukhyang enter your room the other day, and then return to her room secretly holding something. Why don't you search her room?"

"I know Sukhyang's heart is clean as ice and jade. Why would she steal from me?"

Sahyang replied, "She didn't do that in the past. But her marriage proposals have made her act suspiciously even to us maid servants. She seemed to secure property of her own. But I dared not tell you what I saw, because you and the Prime Minister think so highly of her. But now that I've told you the truth, you better inspect her room."

Lady Change grew suspicious of Sukhyang. She called Sukhyang and asked, "Is it true you have the missing articles in your room?"

After some time Sukhyang said: "I didn't bring them to my room. How can the golden hairpin and the ornamental jade knife be in my room?" She took out her household goods and showed them to Lady Chang. Both treasures were in a box of her cosmetic set.

Lady Chang said, angrily, "Why are they here if you didn't take them?"

Lady Chang went to her husband. "We've loved Sukhyang like our own child," she said, "and planned to leave her all our property. But she isn't our child, and she deceived us, keeping our treasures in her own box. How will we handle this?"

Alarmed, Prime Minister Chang said, "I understand how a young lady, infatuated with a golden hairpin, might steal it. But why did she take a jade knife that is no use to her? It's strange. Let's think this matter over."

Standing nearby, Sahyang said, "Sukhyang has lately offered embroidered fabric and her writings to a young man from outside. And he has been covertly sneaking into the house. But I don't know exactly what deals were made."

Furious, Prime Minister Chang said, "If this is so, then she has been intimate with someone outside the house. Letting her stay here any longer will surely bring disaster. You should expel her immediately from our house."

Lady Chang went to Sukhyang's room, where she was lying face down, weeping, with a hairband wrapped about her head, and scolded her: "We grieved day and night over our childlessness and accepted you as our child because your face and conduct were like those of an aristocratic child. We raised you in our arms, loved you like our own child, and entrusted you with overseeing our household affairs. Besides, we made a marriage proposal to a prestigious family to marry you to a good man, and let you take charge of our future affairs. How could you commit such a heavy crime? We are not very rich, but we still own three thousand servants, land that produces tens of thousands of sacks of rice, and enough gold and silver to load on hundreds of thousands of wagons. Don't you think there is enough for you to lead a comfortable life? If you had told me you wanted the golden hairpin, I would have given you a far more precious jewel. I can understand why you stole the golden hairpin, which obsessed you. But why the jade knife, which is no use to you? I have great affection for you, but my husband is very angry. How can I blame him? Stay somewhere nearby until his anger dissolves. I will ask him to forgive you and bring you home." She began to cry.

Sukhyang prostrated herself twice, saying, "My heavy crime in a previous life cost me my parents, and I had to sleep in the bush at night, beg for meals, and endure hunger and cold. But heaven helped me. Thanks to you, I was raised in your precious household with the best clothes and food. I've been treated better than a real child. And since I have nothing more to expect from you, I chose to serve you and perform sincere memorial services for you when you die. I carved it into my mind that, even if I die and my bones turn to soil, I cannot pay back even an infinitesimal fraction of your gifts to me. So how could I harbor the slightest intention to deceive you? I know you would give me whatever I might ask for, like the golden hairpin. Why should I steal something from you? Besides, the ceremonial knife is made for a man; an innocent girl raised in a good family can hardly look at it directly. Do you really think I brought the knife to my room myself? Either someone schemed to cause a rift between us or a mischievous ghost put them in the box of my cosmetic set. Alas, ghosts in heaven and on earth have no words and I have no way to defend myself. So I must kill myself in front of you to prove my innocence. When I die, please think of your old affection for me to dissect my abdomen and hang my body on a pole at the intersection on the street. If even one passer-by understands the falsity of this accusation and clears my name, I may be able to close my eyes and not become an evil spirit, even as I go into the underworld."

Looking at the sky, Sukhyang cried out and prepared to take her life. Lady Chang believing what Sukhyang said, smelled a rat: "Someone tried to entrap Sukhyang."

Fearing that Sukhyang might kill herself, Lady Chang said, "I'm sure you're innocent. I'll tell my husband to soften his anger. Stop feeling sad."

Sukhyang, deeply touched, offered cordial thanks through her tears to the Lady.

Sahyang, eavesdropping, hurried into the room to convey to the Lady a false message from the Prime Minister: "I ordered you to kick Sukhyang out of the house, because I cannot put up with her outrageous conduct. But I heard she is still here. Who dares to oppose my order?" Sahyang said, "He was infuriated. Please send her out of the house immediately."

The grief-stricken Lady sobbed. "Since my husband is still angry, you should pack your dresses and stay for a while in the servants' quarters outside the gate. I will ask him privately tonight to bring you back. Don't be upset anymore."

Sukhyang prostrated herself twice. "I won't be able to repay your benevolence in this world. The scolding you received from the Prime Minister on my account means that I deserve more than ten thousand deaths." Sukhyang again attempted to kill herself.

But the Lady grabbed her hands. "I'm so sad. It's my fault. You've fallen into such dire straits because I told my husband about your wrongdoing without a second thought." She blamed herself, she felt sorry for Sukhyang.

Sahyang returned to say, "The Prime Minister gave me another order: 'An aristocratic child would not behave like this. She must be the child of a man of low birth. If she stays here, she'll bring disaster. Banish her immediately.' He pushed for her to leave again and again."

Sorrier yet, the Lady called a maid servant named Kŭphyang: "Give Sukhyang her dresses and other necessary articles."

Sukhyang wailed. "A few days ago, during a party, an evening magpie flew into me and cried before it left. I thought, 'Heaven has already harmed me enough. What fresh disaster will befall me now?' I am falsely accused. Unable to resist the will of heaven, I have no use for dresses. I'll just take a piece of the jade ring my mother gave me when we parted so that I can cherish it like my mother when I die."

When Sukhyang entered the room, Lady Chang couldn't face her, so she rushed to her husband. "Come to think of it," she said, "I forgot I left the golden hairpin and ornamental jade in Sukhyang's room, and in my temporary madness I suspected Sukhyang. Now she's trying to kill herself. Please forgive my recklessness. Don't be so angry."

Prime Minister Chang said, "Sahyang just reported to me that you're determined to kick Sukhyang out of the house, indignant at her conduct. Consenting to your will, I ordered Sahyang to send her out as soon as possible. But I had no intention of expelling Sukhyang from my house. Do as you please."

Delighted, Lady Chang was about to run to Sukhyang to tell her about his mercy. But he stopped her. "Last night, in a dream, I saw a parrot on a branch of a red peach tree, took it down, and tamed it. Sometime later, a servant cut the branch with an axe before the bird flew away. I don't know what omen this is, but all day my heart has felt empty, as if I had lost something valuable. Can you please ask a lady-in-waiting to bring wine and console me?" Lady Chang asked Kŭphyang to bring him wine and appetizers.

Sahyang, eavesdropping, hurried into Sukhyang's room to say, "The Prime Minister rebuked Lady Chang for 'letting Sukhyang stay in the house' and ordered me to expel you, not to somewhere near but far away. If you don't go soon, I will be punished. Hurry!"

Sukhyang cried, "I will, after bidding farewell to Lady Chang when she returns."

Sahyang scolded Sukhyang. "You committed such a horrendous crime, though you had been given fine dresses and delicious food and caused trouble for Lady Chang. It is shameless for you to think of bidding farewell to her. She, too, is enraged, and doesn't intend to see you. So hurry up! Quick!" Sahyang dragged Sukhyang by the hand.

Sukhyang, biting her finger, wrote in blood her letter of separation on the rice paper window and left the room in tears. Sahyang pushed her to walk faster, cursing her. She pushed Sukhyang's back and dragged her so forcefully by the hand that Sukhyang could hardly walk. Sahyang's rebuke fed her despair, and as she approached the main gate she could not discern the four directions.

Sahyang pushed Sukhyang through the gate. "The Prime Minister is in a bad temper, so don't stay around here. Go as far away as you can. If he hears that you're staying nearby, he'll catch and kill you." Sahyang slammed the door shut and went inside.

Sukhyang Escapes Death; Sahyang Put to Death

Grief-stricken, looking back again and again at the Prime Minister's house, Sukhyang wailed. She wandered aimlessly until she came to a river.

Determined to take her own life, she looked to heaven, sighing, "What crime did I commit in my previous life to suffer this? I lost my parents at five, roamed around in daylight, and slept in groves and bushes at night. After spending days heaving sighs and shedding tears, I was very fortunate to meet Lady Chang, with whom I lived for a decade. Now that I have been falsely accused and kicked out of the house, who shall I rely on now? I'll throw myself into the river without meeting my parents again. I wish the blue sky and a host of celestial bodies would reveal to all the people in the house of Prime Minister Chang, high and low, that I'm innocent!"

Sukhyang cried for a long time, and it was as if heaven and earth were heavyhearted and all the plants and trees and animals were submerged in deep sorrow. Even passers-by stopped and shed tears, feeling pity for her.

The sun had set, birds returned to the forest to sleep, and the leaves falling in the autumn wind added to Sukhyang's woes. Clutching a silk handkerchief in one hand and her skirt in the other, shedding pearl-like teardrops on her jade-like cheeks, she jumped into the water. Mountains and streams, plants and grass, all seemed to shout "No!" and waves turned upside down, beginning to simmer. Alarmed, passers-by desperately tried to save her—to no avail.

Soon five-colored clouds rose from all directions and two fairies with their hair done up in two locks rushed to the scene on the boat of a lotus leaf, shouting, "Princess of the Dragon King! Why don't you pull the lady into the boat?"

A figure resembling a black panel instantly

transformed itself into a pretty girl, who held Sukhyang in her breast and boarded the boat. The fairies prostrated themselves twice to Sukhyang. "Fair lady, why give up your priceless body so indiscreetly? We're on our way to save you, by order of Wŏlgung Hang'a. But we met Master Yŏ Tongbin[44] in the Milky Way, who begged us to bring him more wine. That was why we couldn't come earlier. Your life would be over if not for the princess of the Dragon King."

They thanked the princess and said: "How did you know when to save the girl?"

The princess said, "When the Dragon Kings of the four seas[45] gathered at Crystal Palace[46] for a party in the past, my favorite lady-in-waiting accidently broke a glass. Lest she be punished for this misdemeanor, I didn't report it to my father king. Indignant, he expelled me to the Pan River. Emerging by the riverbank, I was caught by fishermen and was almost eaten. By sheer luck I was saved thanks to the gratitude of Kim Chŏn. But I had not found a way to repay this debt. Just yesterday, right after the Dragon King attended a meeting in Jade Capital[47], the Great Jade Emperor told him,

---

[44] Yŏ Tongbin, or Lü Dongbin (呂洞賓; born 796) in Chinese, was a Tang dynasty poet.

[45] The Four Seas (四海) roughly mean the whole seas of the world or the whole world.

[46] Crystal Palace, or Suchŏng Palace in Korean, is an undersea palace decorated with crystals.

[47] Jade Capital is the fictional capital where the Great Jade

'Wŏlgung Soa, the fairy in the Moon Palace, committed a crime in heaven and has lived in exile in the house of Kim Chŏn in Namyang. She is fated to suffer near-death in succession at the hands of bandits on Mount Panya, in the otherworld of Lady Hut'o, in the P'yojin River, in the field of Hermit Hwadŏk[48], and in a prison in Nagyang. She will undergo more ordeals for another half year before she is reunited with her husband Hermit T'aeŭl, bears him two sons and a daughter, and flourishes.' The Dragon King came down and called the keeper of the waters: 'You must wait and watch the situation closely; when a girl falls into the water, save her.' But I volunteered to save her to repay my gratitude to her father. Now that you two have come, I will leave her to you."

The princess said to Sukhyang, "We will see each other again!" and left.

Failing to grasp the situation, Sukhyang asked the two fairies, "How does that maiden walk on water as if it were the ground?"

One jade fairy said, "She is the third daughter of the Dragon King of the East Sea and the wife of the Dragon King in the P'yojin River. Long ago your father saved her life. So she has come back to rescue you, lady, to repay the favor."

Sukhyang asked again, "Since losing my parents as a child, I lived in the house of another family. But I

Emperor lives.

[48] Hermit Hwadŏk (火德眞君) is the God of Fire.

was expelled from that house after having been falsely accused. I found it hard to continue living in the world, so I decided to jump into the water. Now I humbly thank you for coming to save me and calling me a lady."

One fairy smiled and said, "Perhaps you don't recognize us because you have inhaled filthy odors and have drunk dirty water in the secular world." She offered Sukhyang a cup of dew-like tea. Drinking it, Sukhyang vividly remembered that, as a fairy in the Moon Palace, she had exchanged letters with Hermit T'aeŭl on the face of the Great Jade Emperor and had been exiled to the secular world for stealing the elixir of love to give it to T'aeŭl. Recognizing her own maids from the Moon Palace, Sukhyang was delighted to meet them. The three embraced, weeping with joy.

Sukhyang said, "I know I committed a crime in heaven. Of all the tortures I suffered in the world, separation from my parents and disgrace in Prime Minister Chang's house were most regrettable. I would rather die so that I can forget them all."

The fairy said politely, "No need to worry. Those tragedies were predestined by heaven and thus cannot be undone. For their sins, your parents, too, lost you and are suffering bowel-cutting pain. You, too, were destined to live for only ten years in the house of Prime Minister Chang: no need to lament over that either. Wŏlgung Hang'a knew that Sahyang entrapped you, reported it to the Great Jade Emperor, and allowed her be struck dead by lightning. Prime Minister Chang, his wife, and all the servants in the house know you are innocent. The Prime Minister ordered servants to look for you by the river, to no avail. Don't worry about it. You have suffered three disasters; two more await you. Be careful."

"What misfortunes?"

"You are destined to suffer in a fire in the field of eulalia and imprisonment in Nagyang. After half a year, you will meet Hermit T'aeŭl and enjoy glories ever after."

Sukhyang sighed. "Just thinking of what I have suffered is painful enough. How can I survive the next two trials? Lady Chang loves me and knows I'm innocent, so I would rather go there to avoid these ordeals."

The fairy smiled. "Heaven has already decided your fate. You cannot stop destiny, nor avoid punishment even if it means you have to wear a stone hat and enter a large iron pot of water. First, you were destined to stay in the house of Prime Minister Chang for no more than ten years. Second, if you stay there, you'll never meet Hermit T'aeŭl, because he lives three thousand three hundred and sixty-five *li* from Chang's house. And without the hermit, you will never meet your parents by yourself."

Sukhyang sighed. "You say the hermit came down to the secular world. What's his name?"

The fairy said, "I remember what Wŏlgung Hang'a said long ago: he's the son of Duke Yi in Nagyang, named Yi Sŏn. His pen name is T'aeŭl, and he enjoys wealth, rank, and fame."

"If it's true that both of us committed crimes in

the past and have come down to the secular world, why do I suffer ordeals while he enjoys a beautiful life?"

"You flirted with him first, so your crime is heavier. The Great Jade Emperor had kept the hermit near him and loved him most. He reluctantly consented to exile him into the world because Wŏlgung Hang'a insisted he be punished, too. But he loved the hermit, and so he endowed him with wealth and honor."

"Be that as it may, how could the Emperor be so cruel to me?" she said. "And now that the hermit lives so far away, when can I meet him? Who should I rely on until then? And when will I meet my parents again?"

"Don't worry. You wouldn't get there in a year on foot. But we have prepared a lotus leaf boat, which will take you there in a flash. Magu the Fairy[49] on Mount Ch'ŏnt'ae[50] has come down to the world and waited for a long time for you. You'll have no problem finding someone to rely on. Only after you meet the hermit will you be reunited with your parents." The fairies sang a sailors' song and set the lotus leaf boat afloat. The boat sailed as fast as an arrow.

When they came to a river, one fairy said to Sukhyang, "Now we're at our destination. Please get

---

[49] Magu the Fairy (麻姑; Magu) in Chinese, was a legendary Daoist immortal.

[50] Mount Ch'ŏnt'ae, or Mount Tiantai (天台山) in Chinese, is located in China's Zhejiang Province.

off here and head east. You'll find someone to rescue you." She gave Sukhyang an orange of superior quality and said, "Eat it when you feel hunger on the way." Then they left, grieving the brevity of their meeting.

Scarcely had Sukhyang landed on earth than she looked back and found they were already gone. Perplexed, Sukhyang was at a loss what to do. No sooner did she take two steps to the east than she felt hungry. Eating the orange, she forgot everything in heaven, as if they were the things of time immemorial. She could only remember what she had suffered in the world.

"If a girl wears this gorgeous dress in the street, she might meet disaster." Entering a village, she exchanged her dress for worn-out clothes and painted her face black. Then, pretending to be blind in one eye and limping, she leaned on a stick and went east. Passers-by said to one other, "It's pathetic that such a beautiful girl is sick, with a dark complexion."

* * *

Prime Minister Chang was drinking wine offered by his wife, and when he grew tipsy she said, "These days, because I am more forgetful, I suspected Sukhyang for no reason. After I heard what Sukhyang said, I felt uneasy and very sorry for her."

Alarmed, the Prime Minister said, "Oh my goodness! The poor thing must be tormented. Why don't you ask her to come here so we can console her?"

Just as Lady Chang ordered a lady-in-waiting to call Sukhyang, Sahyang entered the room, pretending to commiserate: "Never have I heard of such an evil deed!"

"What happened?" said Lady Chang.

"We servants long believed Sukhyang must be the child of an aristocratic family. But now she proves to be a child of low birth. No sooner did you enter the Prime Minister's room than Sukhyang wrapped up something and rushed out. Suspicious, I tried to see what it was—in vain—because she ran away. I called after her, 'You should at least bid farewell to the Lady, shouldn't you?' She replied, 'What damn farewell greeting do you say to someone who abused me and kicked me out of the house?' I couldn't catch up with her, because she ran so quickly after the bachelor boy."

Shaken, Lady Chang said, "What are you talking about? I have something to tell her. You must hurry and bring her back without failure!"

Sahyang pretended to hasten her steps in front of the Lady but, when she was out of eyesight, she went to a nearby house. She returned after a while and said, "Sukhyang is already far away. I chased her until I got blisters on my feet and sent your message to her. But she pouted her lips and said in anger, 'With all my beauty and talent, I will find no less precious dresses and food wherever I go, won't I?' Slandering you in every form, she walked shoulder to shoulder with the boy, swinging her arms and laughing, before she disappeared. Even we servants wouldn't behave in such a vulgar way. Sukhyang's filthy and obscene behavior is beyond description."

She had barely finished her false report when a Buddhist monk in a shabby quilted robe entered the house. Prime Minister Chang asked in alarm, "Where are you from? What made you come here?"

Holding his hands together in a Buddhist greeting, the monk said, "I am a heaven-sent monk obeying an order from the Great Jade Emperor. I must distinguish gems from pebbles in this house. Gather everyone, men and women, young and old."

Prime Minister Chang said, "We have nothing to distinguish between good and bad in this house. You must be visiting the wrong house."

"You say there is nothing to distinguish between good and bad? Do you know what happened between Sukhyang and Sahyang?" said the monk.[51]

He could not answer, so Sahyang said, "Prime Minister Chang was enamored of Sukhyang, who begged for food, and raised her in his wife's boudoir like their own child. But Sukhyang committed a hideous crime, stealing an ornamental knife the Emperor bestowed upon the Prime Minister and a golden hairpin he gave to his wife as a wedding present. When she was caught, ashamed, she left the house without saying good-bye, disregarding ten years of gratitude. She went out with a young bachelor boy, exchanging jokes with him. I chased after her, asking her again and again to return, but

---

[51] This paragraph is missing in the original text and is taken from the text in the Ewha Womans University Collection.

she wouldn't listen to me. What a crazy monk you are to accept a bribe from Sukhyang, enter the main quarters of the Prime Minister, and attempt to clear Sukhyang's name with your gibberish? Sir, please order the male servants to scrub his hard watermelon-like skull on the stone floor and drag him out."

The monk laughed. "When you took care of the Prime Minister's household affairs, you stole almost everything you could. But once Sukhyang took charge of the household affairs, stealing became impossible to you. Finally, during a party at the Yŏngch'un Pavilion on March 13 of this year, you stole an ornamental knife and a golden hairpin, put them in a box of the cosmetic set in Sukhyang's room, and told Lady Chang that she took them. You sent a fictitious message from the Prime Minister to his wife to get Sukhyang kicked out, and lied to Lady Chang, after idling your time away at a neighbor's house, when she asked you to bring Sukhyang back. You can cheat Prime Minister and Lady Chang—not heaven!"

He removed a miniature handcart from his sleeve, tossed it into the air, and jumped on it. Heaven and earth shook, as if the sky had fallen. Rain poured down in buckets as it grew dark, lightning flashed everywhere. Prime Minister and Lady Chang and all the servants lay flat, praying for mercy. Then a fireball resembling a big jar fell from the sky and split Sahyang's head apart. Everyone in the house, including the Prime Minister and his wife, fainted.

Lady Chang woke after awhile and said through

her tears, "It's appropriate that Sahyang was punished by Heaven for slandering Sukhyang. But who will Sukhyang rely on now?"

The Lady entered Sukhyang's room and saw that her dresses and articles were intact. She noticed two traces of Sukhyang: a letter written in blood affixed to the window and the moist traces of her tears on the floor. In grief she read the letter:

> *I lost my parents at age five; my crime against heaven must be very serious. I lived for ten years as Prime Minister Chang's family, and my gratitude to the Lady is deep. Waking to find myself in infamy, how can I continue living? Heaven, please resolve my deep sorrow if you are not heartless!"*

Lady Chang sighed. "Sukhyang must have decided to kill herself!" She showed the letter to the Prime Minister, who could not resist his sorrow.

Just then the Prime Minister's nephew, Chang Wŏn, arriving for a visit, heard them talking. He said, "On my way here, I saw a girl praying to heaven and crying in front of the P'yojin River. She must be the girl you're talking about!"

The Prime Minister ordered the servants to bring her back.

The servants inspected the site in front of the P'yojin River and said on their return, "We asked people nearby. They said the girl had fallen into the water and died."

The Prime Minister kept sighing. Lady Chang wailed, repeatedly fainting. The Prime Minister consoled her. "It's no use crying over the death even of one's own child. No need to fret over the death of another's child."

"When Sukhyang was with us, everything was beautiful. After she left, only her seats and the image of her movement linger before my eyes and her voice rings in my ears to break my heartstrings. How can I calm down?"

Afraid his wife might get sick, the Prime Minister thought, "She may stop wailing if I hire a painter to draw a portrait of Sukhyang." He sought out a talented artist.

The servant Chang Chŏk said to the Prime Minister, "I once carried Sukhyang on my back to the Noryu Pavilion to enjoy a game of swing before she turned ten. There a painter named Cho Chang from Changsa[52] saw Sukhyang and said, 'I have seen all the women of peerless beauty across the country, but never have I seen such a beautiful one as this girl.' He drew a portrait of her and left. If you find him, you'll get her portrait."

Pleased, the Prime Minister ordered Chang Chŏk to find the artist to acquire the picture. When Chang met Cho, the artist said, "I already sold it to someone."

When Chang Chŏk returned empty-handed, the

---

[52] Changsa, or Changsha (長沙) in Chinese, is the capital of Hunan Province.

Prime Minister said, "Go see him again and ask him to sell it to me for twice as much."

Chang Chŏk took the Prime Minister's message to the artist, who finally sold him the drawing. It was as if Sukhyang had returned alive. Lady Chang was so glad she rolled around on the floor, wailing, clutching the portrait to her breast. She hung it on the wall, prepared boiled rice for it mornings and evenings, as if she were alive, and daily grieved for her.

Sukhyang Meets New Helpers

After parting with the fairies of the Moon Palace, Sukhyang passed herself off as a cripple aimlessly walking east. Not knowing what to do after dark on the road, she grew helpless. Staring ahead, she saw a field of eulalia stretching in every direction. There was no tall tree nearby, so she slept on a shrub of eulalia. A strong gust of wind blew that night, igniting the field. Fire spread everywhere, reaching into the sky.

Perplexed, Sukhyang looked to heaven and said, "I barely survived all sorts of hardship, hoping to be reunited with my parents, and now I'll die in a fire. I don't care about dying, but the thought of never seeing my parents again is spine-shattering."

As she wept, an old man with a stick appeared from the south. "What kind of girl are you," he said, "to come here in the dead of night to meet fire?"

Sukhyang prayed to him: "I'm an orphan, I've wandered everywhere, and with no one to rely on I took a wrong turn. Now I will be burned to death.

Please help me!"

The old man said, "I know your name even without you telling me. With the fire so near, you should take off your clothes and leave them here. Ride on my back."

Sukhyang had to follow his suggestion and rode naked on his back. The fire burned up the dress she had just taken off. The old man removed a red fan from his sleeve and waved it. The fire died back. After crossing the field of eulalia with Sukhyang on his back, the old man tore off part of his sleeve and gave it to her. "Use this to cover the lower half of your body and head east. Now that you've avoided fire, you will triumph. Don't forget my gratitude."

Sukhyang offered cordial thanks. "Where do you live? What's your name?"

"I live in the second house outside the Southern Heaven Gate in heaven, and I am called Hermit Hwadŏk. If not for me, how could you cross a field of eulalia three hundred *li* wide and avoid the fire?" The old man vanished.

* * *

The day had dawned bright when Sukhyang walked eastward, naked and weeping. Her feet were sore. She was hungry and had no choice but to enter a bush under a tree by the road and cover her front with the sleeve-cloth Hermit Hwadŏk had given her.

Then she saw an old woman holding a bamboo basket, who sat down next to her. "What kind of girl are you," she said, "who strips herself and weeps in the street? Did you commit a crime against your parents? Were you kicked out of the house? Did you steal possessions of others and flee? Did you meet hooligans who took your clothes? Or did you sleep in a neighbor's house and escape a fire? What happened?"

Sukhyang said, "I'm a beggar with no parents. I've never been kicked out of a house, or stolen someone's possessions, or slept in another house, or met hooligans. But I'm sitting here, newly impoverished."

The old woman laughed. "If you're parentless, how were you born? Did you fall out of heaven or spring from the earth? To be deserted by your parents is different than being abandoned, isn't it? Is leaving the house of Prime Minister Chang, accused of stealing a hairpin and a knife different from being charged with theft and kicked out? Is having your clothes burned up in the field of eulalia different than meeting hooligans?"

Sukhyang was alarmed. "How do you know these details so precisely?"

The old woman laughed. "I heard them through the grapevine. Where are you going?"

"I have no destination. And since I'm stark naked, I can't go anywhere."

"Then how about living with me? I'm a widow living without a child."

"If you don't desert me, I'll follow you. But even if I knew where you live, it isn't likely that I can budge now. I'm naked and starving to death."

The old woman took some boiled vegetables from

her basket. "Eat these." Sukhyang was soon stuffed and grew energetic, her body smelling fragrant.

The old woman took off her outer garment and gave it to Sukhyang. "Wear this and follow me." Sukhyang put on the dress and followed the old woman over two passes. She saw many houses in a row in a highly peaceful village. After passing the village, the two arrived at the base of a big mountain.

The old woman said, "You'll live here with me from now on."

The house was not grandiose but clean. Household goods were few but neatly arranged. There were no other living creatures save a blue *sapsari*[53] that resembled a lion. It greeted her, wagging its tail as it did for its former master.

Half a month passed, with Sukhyang still pretending to be a cripple. One day the old woman said, "Your face looks like the autumn moon shrouded in dark clouds. You don't look handicapped. You'd better stop deceiving me." Sukhyang smiled without speaking.

Before leaving, the old woman said, "I sell wine here, so village people frequent this house. I'm afraid they'll think you're filthy. I hope you wash your face,

---

[53] *Sapsari*, or *sapsal-gae*, is a shaggy Korean breed of dog. The word is a compound of *sapsal* and the suffix *i* (hypocorism) or *gae* (dog). Similar to the English sheepdog in appearance, the breed is also called "a lion dog" for its luxurious coat of soft shaggy hair and its intrepid spirit and is believed to "dispel or ward off" (*sap* in old Korean) evil spirits (*sal*). The breed was designated as Korean Natural Monument No. 368.

at the least."

She checked the house for many days, finding no special man. Some villagers frequented it, but never indiscreetly. Relieved, Sukhyang washed her face, exchanged her dress for a new one, and leaned against the window, embroidering figures.

After a while, the old woman entered the room and was surprised. "Dear me, you are really beautiful. What crime did you commit in your previous life in heaven so that you had to leave the Kwanghan Hall[54] and suffer ordeals in the secular world?"

Sukhyang sighed. "Because you love me like your own child, how can I deceive you? I was born to an aristocratic family. During a bandit riot, I lost my parents and wandered with no particular destination in mind. Then a deer carried me on its back to the house of Prime Minister Chang. I lived there for ten years until a maid servant named Sahyang slandered me. I had no other choice but to jump into the P'yojin River, but lotus flower-digging children saved me. They said to me to head east, so I walked in that direction aimlessly. When I met fire in the field of eulalia and almost died, an old man, Hermit Hwadŏk, saved me. Then I met you, and here am I. Because you love me like your own child, I will serve you like my mother. Please treat me as your daughter. I hope we don't deceive each other. I'm afraid that men will harass me in the same way that voluptuous

---

[54] Kwanghan Hall (廣寒殿; Guanghandian in Chinese) is a pavilion where Wŏlgung Hang'a lives in the Moon Palace.

butterflies and crazy honeybees covet flowers."

The old woman adjusted her dress, went down to the garden, and prostrated herself to Sukhyang. "Young lady, you don't need to say that. How could I deceive you and ruin your life? You don't need to be afraid of anything."

From that day on the old woman was more polite. Sukhyang was conversant with worldly affairs, clever, and extraordinarily skilled, especially in embroidery. Her fabrics fetched generous prices, making the old woman richer.

Sukhyang's Encounter with Yi Sŏn

On the fifteenth day of next March, the old woman went out to sell wine, and Sukhyang was embroidering designs alone when a bluebird alighted on a branch of an apricot tree and wept. Sukhyang said, "Perhaps the bird lost its parents like me? Why else does it weep alone?"

She dozed off weeping. The bluebird said, "Your parents are over there. Follow me."

Sukhyang followed it to a pond clear as white jade, where a pavilion was propped up by columns of beads, with cornerstones and pillars made of agate and amber, and a roof of glass. Dazzled, she could not look at it directly. "Yoji,"[55] written in gold on the

---

[55] Yoji, or Yaochi (瑤池) in Chinese, is the Jade Lake on Mount Kolloyun, or Mount Kunlun (崑崙山) in Chinese. It is the residence of Sŏ Wangmo, or Xi Wangmu (西王母).

coral signboard, suggested it was Sŏ Wangmo's [56] residence, which prompted Sukhyang to stay outside.

All at once five-colored clouds rose in the west, a mysterious fragrance filled the air, and countless hermit officers and fairies entered in pairs riding on the backs of dragons and phoenixes. Shrouded in blue clouds, the Great Jade Emperor rode in a jade wagon carried by six dragons and escorted by the Shakyamuni Buddha from India, all the heavenly gods and Buddhas[57], the Three Terraces[58], the Big Dipper, Avalokitesvara Bodhisattva, *arhats*[59], and other bodhisattvas. When the solemn procession went through the door with music ringing from all directions, it produced a magnificent spectacle. They took no heed of Sukhyang.

With clouds rising, many fairies carried in a white jade palanquin, where the supreme fairy sat, holding a white lotus flower. She was Wŏlgung Hang'a.

She said to Sukhyang. "I'm so happy to see you,

---

[56] Sŏ Wangmo, or Xi Wangmu (西王母) in Chinese, is the Queen Mother of the West, an ancient Chinese goddess.

[57] Buddha can either refer to the historical Shakyamuni Buddha or to anyone who has attained full enlightenment. In general, 'Buddha' means "awakened one, someone who has wakened from the sleep of ignorance and sees things as they really are. Buddha also refers to someone who is completely free from all faults and mental obstructions.

[58] The Three Terraces, Santai (三台) in Chinese, are the three pairs of stars in Ursa Major.

[59] Buddhism denotes *arhat* (Sanskrit) as an enlightened person who has attained *nirvana*.

Soa[60]! What hardship have you suffered in the secular world? Why don't you come with me to look at the scenery of Yoji."

Sukhyang followed Hang'a into the house whose stylish form and imposing grandeur were beyond description. With various kinds of music reverberating in the air, a hermit, preceded by a hermit officer, entered the hall and met the Great Jade Emperor. The Emperor said, "My dear T'aeŭl, how do you like the secular world? Have you met Soa?" T'aeŭl lay face down on the ground, apologizing for his past crimes.

Wŏlgung Hang'a said to the Great Jade Emperor, "As Soa has suffered near-death four times now, please make a decision about her fortune."

Consenting to this proposal, the Great Jade Emperor asked the Shakyamuni Buddha to determine Soa's life span. Shakyamuni replied, "I propose seventy years."

The Great Jade Emperor asked the Big Dipper to decide how many children she would have. The Big Dipper replied, "I suggest two sons and a daughter."

The Great Jade Emperor asked the South Big Dipper to set her children's government posts. The South Big Dipper said, "I hope both sons will become Prime Minister and the daughter will be the Empress."

Then the Great Jade Emperor asked Soa to give Hermit T'aeŭl two heavenly peaches and a flower

---

[60] Soa means moon, but in this context it refers to Sukhyang, who was named Wŏlgung Soa (Soa in the Moon Palace).

from a cinnamon tree. Soa, holding a jade tray with two peaches in one hand and a cinnamon tree flower in the other, gave them to Hermit T'aeŭl. He carefully observed her as he received them. Her face flushed, she was about to turn back when the pearl of her jade ring touched the cinnamon flower and fell to the ground. She was bending over to pick it up when the hermit officer caught it. Ashamed, Soa was ready to return to the building when the old woman woke her. "The spring days must have tired you out. How could you nap for so long!" Upon hearing her voice, Sukhyang came awake.

Sitting up, Sukhyang saw the landscape of Yoji lingering before her eyes, with the music of heaven still ringing in her ears.

The old woman said, "How was heaven different from the human world?"

Taken by surprise, Sukhyang said, "How do you know that I saw heaven in my dream?"

The old woman laughed. "You followed a blue bird, didn't you? The bird told me."

Shocked, Sukhyang retold her dream. The old woman said, "After seeing such a marvelous spectacle, you shouldn't keep it in your memory. Why not embroider it for posterity?"

Her suggestion made sense, so Sukhyang embroidered on fabric what she had seen in heaven. Astonished, the old woman said, "Your talent is truly unparalleled across all ages. How about selling this picture to anyone who could really understand its real value?"

"I know the actual scene is more valuable than ten

thousand *nyang*⁶¹ in gold coins; a thousand *nyang* in gold coins would not reward my devotion. But who among the earthly people can recognize its value? You may as well sell it to anyone who would give us fifty pieces of gold."

The old woman laughed. "Who would pay fifty *nyang* in gold coins for a two *cha*-long⁶² silk? But let's give it a try!"

The old woman showed the painting to customers in the market but no one recognized its value. Then a certain Cho Chang living in Changsa, a man with a discerning eye, asked the old woman, "Where did you get this embroidered silk?"

"My little daughter embroidered it. Why do you ask?"

"Where do you live?"

"I sell wine at the Yihwa Public House in Bukchon, in Nagyang⁶³."

When Cho Chang again asked the price, she replied, "You tell me." Cho Chang said, "The actual scenery is worth more than ten thousand *nyang* in gold coins, and her devotion is worth more than a thousand *nyang* in gold coins. I will at least pay the price of her sincerity."

---

⁶¹ *Nyang* is a unit of old Korean coinage. The exact value of 1 *nyang* varied according to the times, but in late Chosŏn dynasty one sack of rice, 144kg, cost five *nyang*. Thus in current terms one *nyang* was approximately $70.

⁶² *Cha* is a unit of measurement. One *cha* equals 30.3 cm.

⁶³ Nagyang, or Luoyang (洛陽) in Chinese, is a city in Henan Province.

Delivering a thousand *nyang* in gold coins to the old woman, he said, "Who on earth knows the value of this picture? It portrays Sŏ Wangmo offering heavenly peaches to the Great Jade Emperor at a banquet in Yoji, in heaven. How could this be your daughter's work?" He left with the picture. "This very gifted figure was surely born in the world."

Upon her return home, the old woman told this story to Sukhyang, who said, in admiration, "I'm surprised that someone cherishes the genuine artifact in the world." The old woman used the gold coins to buy Sukhyang's dresses and household things.

Pleased with his precious embroidery, Cho Chang looked everywhere for the most gifted man of letters and calligraphy to write about and title the picture. One day he heard that Yi Sŏn, the young son of Duke Yi of Wi[64] in Northern Village in Nagyang, was a more talented writer than Yi Chŏkson and Tu Mokchi[65] and outdid even Wang Hŭiji and Cho Maengpu in calligraphy. After preparing gifts, Cho went to Northern Village in Nagyang to meet him.

* * *

In Northern Village in Nagyang lived a man named Yi Chŏng, who was skilled in writing and martial arts

---

[64] Wi, or Wei (魏) in Chinese, is the name of a country.

[65] Tu Mokchi, or Du Mu (杜牧; 803–852) in Chinese, was an acclaimed Tang dynasty poet.

from childhood. He passed the state-run civil service examination and rendered distinguished services for the nation many times as Minister of National Defense. In tribute to his achievement, the Emperor appointed him Duke[66] of Wi, entrusting him with all state affairs. Lest he should be embroiled in political disputes, however, Yi returned to his hometown, feigning sickness. The Emperor, cherishing his loyalty and talent, did not deprive him of his position as Duke of Wi and entrusted him with overseeing military affairs. Duke Yi acted with dignity throughout the country, accumulating almost as much gold and silver as the Emperor. But he daily lamented his childlessness.

On the fifteenth of July, in the Year of Muja, Duke Yi and his wife climbed the stairs of the Manwŏl Pavilion to gaze at the moon.

He said, "Our wealth is unparalleled among court officials, and your beauty and talent is unrivaled in the world. But we have no child yet. Who will burn incense for the ancestral rites in our family? As a high government official, I may have two wives, and so I want to find another wife. Please do not feel bitter over my heartlessness."

Lady Yi felt sorrow, saying "Given your prestige, you deserve ten wives or even more. But what if we have no child not because of me but you?"

The Duke laughed. "When I fail to have a child with another wife, I will blame no one."

---

[66] Duke was the highest of the five peerage titles in old China.

Lady Yi was the daughter of Vice Premier Wang P'ae. Her husband's plan to marry another woman made her toss and turn all night. She went to her parents' house the next day and said, "Because I haven't borne a child, my husband wants a new wife. What shall I do?"

Wang P'ae said, "Of the three thousand crimes of disobedient children, they say, failing to beget a child is the most serious. How can you blame him for your bad luck?"

Her mother said, "They say the Buddha at the Taesŏng Temple performs extraordinary miracles. Some childless couples who sincerely prayed there bore children, they say. Why don't you go there and pray with all your heart and soul?"

Hearing this, Lady Yi performed ablutions and purified herself. She prayed earnestly for a baby at the Taesŏng Temple and then returned to her parents' house.

That night a Buddhist monk appeared in her dream. "Your husband, the Duke, is destined to have no child not because he committed a crime in his last life but because he killed so many innocent people, taking pleasure in punishing others. But your sincere devotion has impressed heaven, so I will allow you to bear a child. Please return home immediately."

Waking from sleep, Lady Yi prayed to heaven, bid farewell to her parents, and went home. The Duke said, "Why do you come home after so many days away?"

"You underestimated me. I prayed to heaven for

our offspring," she said, smiling.

The Duke laughed. "If one could have a child by praying to heaven, no married woman would remain childless."

She countered, "If a wife can be kicked out of the house for bearing no child, no childless wife would live with her husband." Thus they continued joking.

That night the Duke dreamed that with five-colored clouds unfolding, a young hermit officer in red attire with a hat[67] descended with a jade scepter in his hand; after bowing twice, he said, "I am Hermit T'aeŭl who used to serve the Great Jade Emperor. After committing a crime against the Emperor in heaven, I was exiled into the world. As I wandered here and there with no destination in mind, the Buddha at the Taesŏng Temple guided me to this house. So please be kind to me."

Waking from this dream, the Duke rushed into his wife's boudoir and said, "I remember you told me you prayed for a child. Was it at the Taesŏng Temple?"

Lady Yi was quite surprised. "How did you know?"

He told her what he had heard in his dream. Intrigued, Lady Yi said she prayed for a child at the Taesŏng Temple, and the Buddha prophesied her pregnancy. He thought it was marvelous.

From then on she began to show signs of her pregnancy. Time passed. It was the Buddha's

---

[67] Red attire on a hat signals that the wearer is a high officer above rank three.

Birthday in April, in the Year of Kich'uk. The Duke had gone to the capital, so she was home alone. Five-colored clouds encircled the house, and a mysterious fragrance spread around it. Finding this strange, she ordered her ladies-in-waiting to sweep the house. She felt tired that afternoon and dozed off on her bed. When she heard a crane cry outside the window, two fairies entered the room, saying, "The time has come. Please lie down and feel at home."

They undressed her, and soon she bore a son. The fairies washed the baby with fragrant water in a jade bottle before hurrying out of the room.

"Why are you leaving so quickly after rendering services with sincerity?" Lady Yi asked. "Please tell me who you are. I will express my gratitude to you."

"We are the fairies in charge of childbirth. We came to help you deliver your baby by order of the Great Jade Emperor. And we must hurry because the future wife of this baby is about to be born in Namyang."

Lady Yi said, "I am very grateful to you, fairies, for coming down to the filthy secular world for me. But tell me who will become his wife? Who are her parents?"

"She was named Wŏlgung Soa in her previous life. In this world she is named Sukhyang, daughter of Kim Chŏn, who lives in Namyang," they said, and disappeared. Lady Yi ordered her ladies-in-waiting to bring a brush and ink and recorded what the fairies said.

That same day Duke Yi was sleeping in his quarters after completing his duties at the palace. In a dream, he saw his wife struck by lightning. Waking, surprised, he described his dream to the Emperor at the regular assembly, and before he could return to his quarters the Emperor said, "Has your wife been pregnant?"

Duke Yi replied, "Yes, she is carrying a new life."

The Emperor was quite pleased. "In my astronomical observations last night I saw that the Star of T'aeŭl had fallen on Northern Village in Nagyang. I thought a great person will be born there, and it's your son. Please raise him with the utmost care as a future leader who will bring prosperity to the nation."

Duke Yi thanked the Emperor for his blessing, then returned home to find his wife had given birth to a precious boy. Satisfied, he rushed into his wife's boudoir and saw the baby, who had the face of the hermit officer he saw in his dream. Duke Yi named him Sŏn; T'aeŭl was his pen name. The next day he sent a letter reporting his son's birth to the Emperor, who was very pleased, gave many prizes, and promoted the Duke and his wife.

Yi Sŏn walked by the age of one and grew plump. At two, he learned to speak well enough to compete with So Chin[68] and Chang Ŭi[69]. By three, he had a sense of filial piety, friendship, loyalty to the nation,

---

[68] So Chin, or Su Qin (蘇秦; 380-284 BC) in Chinese, was a noted strategist in the Warring States period.

[69] Chang Ŭi, or Zhang Yi (張儀; 329-309 BC) in Chinese, was a noted strategist in the Warring States period.

and sincerity. He learned letters at four and knew everything he studied. At five, he memorized writings he had never read. At seven, even a world-famous writer could not outdo Yi. Thus people said, "It must be the rebirth of Tu Mokchi."

Growing up, Yi would joke, "I will marry no one but the fairy of the Moon Palace."

One day Sŏn said to Duke Yi, "I heard they will soon hold a state-run civil service examination. I hope I can apply for it."

Duke Yi said, "I know your talent is not dwarfed by Yi Chŏkson so you will certainly pass the examination. But remember that people who succeed early in life are likely to die young. And it will be hard for us to meet once you get a government post—an intolerable pain for us. So you should wait for the next opportunity." Sŏn gave up his plan to take the examination.

* * *

Yi Sŏn found his daily life so monotonous that he would often gaze at the nearby mountains and waters. On the fifteenth day of March, he went to the Taesŏng Temple. Feeling tired, he leaned against the banisters and fell asleep.

A Buddha appeared in a dream to say, "Sŏ Wangmo is hosting a banquet today in Yoji. Why don't you follow me to see the party?" Yi happily followed the Buddha to a spot, where countless fairies gathered and moved about busily. The magnificent pavilion, surrounded by five-colored clouds, with fragrant aromas filling the air, was beyond description.

The Buddha, pointing, said, "Can you see it? Seated on the Jade Pavilion in the north is the Great Jade Emperor. Behind him are the Three Terraces and the Big Dipper, which govern the movements of the stars. On the White Jade Bridge in the east is seated Shakyamuni Buddha, attended by other Buddhas. I will enter the pavilion first. Follow me. You should greet the Great Jade Emperor first and then meet the hermit officers on either side of him.

"It is so magnificent I can't distinguish east from west," Yi said.

The Buddha removed from his sleeve a jujube-like fruit. "Eat this and you will see what really happens."

After eating it, Yi remembered what happened in his last life, as if it had occurred only yesterday. There were all the hermit officers who had been his close friends. Unable to hide his delight at this reunion, Yi gave thanks to the Buddha and followed him inside to prostrate to the Great Jade Emperor, then said hello to the hermit officers, who warmly greeted him.

The Great Jade Emperor asked Yi, "How are you, T'aeŭl? How is life in the world? Have you met Soa?"

Yi lay face down to apologize for his past wrongdoings. The Great Jade Emperor ordered a fairy to give him two pears and a flower from a cinnamon tree. He accepted them, furtively glancing at the fairy. Ashamed, she turned back when a pearl on her jade ring touched the cinnamon flower and fell to the ground. Yi picked it up and was about to tease her.

At that moment he heard the ringing of a bell struck by monks at the Taesŏng Temple to herald the evening offering to Buddha. Waking from sleep, Yi saw the scene in Yoji still before his eyes, and the heavenly music rang in his ears. He noticed he was still holding in his hand the pearl in the dream. Intrigued, he sat down to write an essay about what he had seen in dream, bade farewell to the Buddha at the temple, and returned home. From then on Yi thought only of Soa, indifferent to wealth, rank, and fame, consoling himself by doing calligraphy.

One day a boy running an errand said to him, "A man named Cho Chang from Changsa has brought a piece of silk. He wants to meet you."

Yi ordered the boy to bring him in. Cho prostrated himself. "I acquired a masterpiece of embroidery and searched for a master writer and calligrapher to title it. I heard you are second to none in writing, so I have traveled a great distance. Please write something for the painting."

Cho spread it out. He recognized it as a drawing of Yoji, which he had seen in his dream. Yi was astonished. "Where did you get it?"

Cho was afraid the old woman had stolen the drawing from Yi's house. "Why are you so surprised to see this drawing?"

"It's such a great drawing, fit for a scholar, though it is nothing but a piece of scrap paper to you. I have a masterpiece picture scroll. How about exchanging it for mine? Or I will pay you a generous price for it. Please sell it to me."

"I'm a dealer seeking profit. I paid a thousand *nyang* in gold coins for it. I'll sell it to you if you give me twice the price."

Yi bought the drawing for two thousand *nyang* in gold coins. He wrote his recollections of Yoji in gold letters and hung the scroll in his bedroom. When he saw the drawing every morning and night, he felt as if he were in Yoji, though he still lived in the world. Thenceforth he thought only of finding Soa, losing all interest in other worldly affairs.

Yi Sŏn Searches for Sukhyang

One day Yi Sŏn recognized something mysterious. "I visited Yoji in my dream. But what kind of person was the artist who in the secular world could embroider so precisely the celestial scene? The artist must be an extraordinary person. I must see this artist even though I may not be filial to my parents," he told himself.

He set out on a journey the next morning. "Cho Chang said he bought this from an old woman who sells wine in the Yihwa Public House in Eastern Village in Nagyang. I must go there and ask her." He hurried to the public house.

At that time Sukhyang was embroidering a design on fabric in the pavilion in the Yihwa Public House, when a blue bird, with a pomegranate flower in its beak, flew in front of her and then north again. Curious, Sukhyang raised the bead curtain and looked north, toward the bird. A boy riding a white mule, wearing a turban and a green silk summer jacket, was approaching her house. Looking closer, Sukhyang thought he resembled the hermit officer to whom she gave peaches in Yoji. Pleased and surprised, she dropped the bead curtains and sat still.

After a while the boy arrived at the gate of the Yihwa Public House. "Is anyone here?"

The old woman came out and recognized the boy as the son of Duke Yi in Northern Village. She greeted him, led him to a reception room, and asked him to take a seat. "It is a great honor for a young noble like you to visit such a humble house."

"I just dropped in while passing by because I heard the taste of wine here is excellent. Please don't hesitate to treat me to your wine," Student Yi[70] said.

Laughing, the old woman said, "The wine in our house is ripe and delicious, but I can't drink it because I have no wine friend. Thank heaven you came today. Please help yourself."

She went into the kitchen, and returned with a small portable dining table inlaid with mother-of-pearl on which were five-colored bowls containing a variety of foods rarely found in the secular world. Yi asked her about the extraordinary bowls and food as she drank.

Half tipsy, she laughed. "You're the noble son of Duke Yi. You must be familiar with all sorts of

---

[70] Student Yi is the translation of Yi Saeng (李生). Yi is the last name of Yi Sŏn. Saeng (生), used as a title, means a student at a Confucian academy. The original text used both Yi Sŏn and Yi Saeng alternately.

sumptuous meals and delicacies. But you may not have tried the coarse food of a county house like this. I hope you just taste them."

"I feel uneasy over eating food that I haven't tasted in the secular world. So I must ask you what they are before I eat them."

"I was lazy, so I borrowed them from my neighbors. How can I know them all?"

"Old classics say, 'You should not eat anything without knowing what it is.' Thus I will not eat them until I know their sources."

The old woman laughed and said reluctantly, "I acquired glow-in-the-dark plants in the glass from the underwater palace of the Dragon King in the East Sea, diamond plants in the coral vessel from Hermit Kuru on Mount Yŏngju, mysterious gleaming plants in an amber vessel from Old Magu the Fairy on Mount Ch'ŏnt'ae, heavenly plants in a sea turtle shell dish from a hermit on Mount Mansu, and peaches in an agate vessel from Sŏ Wangmo in Yoji. The foods here are coarse and plain, but they won't hurt you. You must believe me."

Yi grew more suspicious. "Your fancy words seem far from the truth. You live in the world, but the underwater palace of the Dragon King, Mount Yŏngju, Mount Mansu, Mount Ch'ŏnt'ae, and Yoji are all fairylands. Even the First Emperor of Qin[71]

---

[71] The First Emperor of Qin, or Qin Shi Huang (秦始皇; 259–210 BC) in Chinese, was the first emperor to unify China.

and Emperor Mu of Han [72] failed to see those enchanted gardens, with all their powers. How are you able to visit these places?"

"I am old and weak, but I can go wherever I like, whether the four seas or eight directions at my disposal. I won't be guided by someone like you."

"I have a mule that can walk a thousand *li*[73]. So I can. And I do not need guides like you."

She laughed loudly. "If you have such a great mule, why did you follow the Buddha in the Taesŏng Temple on foot to visit Yoji?"

Realizing that she was an extraordinary woman, Yi rose to his feet and prostrated himself to her. "Your words are true in every way. But how did you know I visited Yoji in a dream."

The old woman laughed. "What did you do with the peaches and the flower of a cinnamon tree offered by the Great Jade Emperor in heaven? Did you meet Wŏlgung Soa?"

"A dream is hollow, you know. I don't remember anything."

"If you say it was hollow, it may be so. But was it a dream you bought an embroidered silk from Cho Chang?"

---

[72] Emperor Mu (漢武帝; 157-87 BC), or Emperor Wu of Han in Chinese, was the seventh emperor of the Han dynasty.

[73] One thousand *li* in Korean is an idiomatic way of denoting a long distance rather than an actual physical distance. One *li* equals 0.393 km. This expression often appears in this fiction.

Yi stood up again and prostrated himself twice. "Because I am a man of vulgar taste in the world, I failed to recognize your noble presence and made a bunch of mistakes. I apologize to you sincerely for my rudeness. When I heard that Soa has come down to the world, I came here to look for her. Please don't play a trick on me. Tell me where she is."

She said with a frown, "I know where Soa is. But why are you looking for her?"

"Soa is my heaven-sent wife. Help me meet her."

"If you ever hope to marry her, you must stop searching for her."

"Does she have a problem?"

"You are the noble son of Duke of Yi and stand second to none in family honor and wealth. Thus you deserve the title of son-in-law to the Emperor or at least the highest-ranking officials. Why are you attempting to marry a woman like Soa?"

He was more curious. "Does she have any shortcomings?"

She said with a smile, "She committed a crime in heaven and thus became the daughter of a commoner. She lost her parents at five during the bandit riot and wandered here and there as a beggar. She lost one arm to a bandit's sword, fell into the P'yojin River but was saved by a passer-by, and thenceforth became an amaurotic. After meeting with fire in a field of eulalia, she had one leg burned and now limps. Worse, she lost her hearing after trifling with the spirit of the Shrine to Lady Hut'o. How can a nobleman like you marry such a handicapped person on earth? Your words sound hollow to me."

"What crime did she commit in heaven that caused her to suffer such ordeals?"

"They say that in her previous life Soa attended the Great Jade Emperor as a fairy in the Moon Palace. She stole two elixirs of life and gave them to Hermit T'aeŭl. As punishment, she now lives in exile in the human world."

Yi sighed. "If we are a match predestined in heaven, how can I distinguish between rich and poor? Even if she is handicapped, how can I desert her?"

"You may seek her with all your heart and soul, but your father will never accept her as his daughter-in-law. It's no use trying."

Yi looked at the sky and vowed, "My parents don't understand my intention and try to make me a son-in-law of the Emperor, but I won't marry anyone but Soa. Please do me a favor and tell me where she is. I will repay your gratitude even after I die."

"It's been a long time since Soa and I were separated. I don't know her whereabouts precisely. You must visit the house of Kim Chŏn in Namyang; if you can't find her there, go to the house of Prime Minister Chang in Namgun. Soa is named Sukhyang in the world. Please find her with your heart and soul."

Yi prostrated himself to the old woman twice before bidding farewell.

* * *

He lied to his parents when he got home. "I heard a gifted writer was born in Hyŏngch'o. Renowned scholars from across the nation are flocking to see him. I want to visit him."

Parting with his parents, he carried one hundred *nyang* in gold coins around his waist and rode his mule to Namyang. When he arrived at Kim Chŏn's house, an old man came out to greet him.

Yi said, "I'm the son of Duke Yi of Wi in Northern Village in Nagyang. I've come to meet Kim Chŏn."

"Kim Chŏn is the son of Master Unsu," said the old man. "The Emperor wanted the son of a virtuous man working for the government and assigned him to the governorship of Nagyang. He's not here. I'm afraid you won't meet him. What made you come here?"

"I heard that Sukhyang lives in this house."

"Sukhyang is Kim's daughter. But Kim lost her when she was five, during a riot on Mount Panya. Nobody knows weather she's alive or dead."

"Who are you?"

"I'm the servant who takes care of this house."

Yi left for Namgun, sending word of his arrival to the gate at the house of Prime Minister Chang, who came right out to greet him. The two took their seats.

"Where did you come from? What makes such a nobleman as you journey to this humble house?" the Prime Minister asked.

Yi prostrated himself to the Prime Minister. "I'm the son of Duke Yi of Wi in Northern Village in Nagyang. I heard that Sukhyang, the daughter of Kim Chŏn in Namyang, is a heaven-sent match for me, and since she lives in your house I have come to make a marriage proposal. Please let me marry her."

Prime Minister Chang burst into tears. "When Sukhyang was five years old, a deer carried her on its back to my garden. We had no children, so we raised her for ten years as our own daughter. But as luck would have it, a maid servant named Sahyang slandered her, and I kicked her out of my house. We later heard that Sukhyang went to the P'yojin River to take her life. I ordered the servants to search for her—in vain. We are still in mourning."

"I came a long way after hearing that Sukhyang lives here. Humble as I am, I will respect you and will not disappoint you. Please don't reject my proposal of marriage."

"Even if Sukhyang were my real daughter, I would not dare to hope to be related by marriage to the Duke of Wi. It would be my great honor for Sukhyang to become the Duke's daughter-in-law. Judging from your appearance and attitude, I think you deserve to be her husband. But it is our misfortune to have lost her. And it is no use lamenting this."

"I heard that Sukhyang cannot walk very fast, since she's crippled. Where could she go by herself, after being abused by Sahyang?"

Prime Minister Chang said, "My wife's grief over Sukhyang was so profound that I bought her a portrait of the girl for a thousand *nyang* in gold coins and hung it in her boudoir. She gazes at it day and night, as if Sukhyang were still alive[74]. Follow me to

---

[74] Half of this line in the original text was erased and cannot

see it for yourself."

Prime Minister Chang led Yi by hand to his wife's room. When Yi saw the portrait of a girl holding a peony blossom—the fairy from his dream—he couldn't hide his joy.

"I heard she was crippled, but I find no trace of any handicap. What happened?" Yi said.

"Sukhyang wasn't born that way. The painting was done before she was ten, after which she grew even more beautiful."

"I've come a long way to meet her but now must return home. Please sell me her painting."

"I recognize your sincerity. I would have given you the painting for free if it didn't belong to my wife. But she would be as good as dead without it. I'm sorry, I can't sell it to you"

Yi helplessly bade farewell to Prime Minister Chang. He visited the P'yojin River on his way home to search for Sukhyang. No one knew her whereabouts. Then an old man appeared. "Years ago," he said, "a girl such as you describe came from Prime Minister Chang's house and wept on this very spot, saying, 'I was entrapped by Sahyang and now have a bad reputation. I will die an untimely death.' Then she fell into the water and drowned."

Unable to resist his sorrow, he sold the gold he had on him to buy incense, candles, and other ritual offerings. When he wrote an ode for the dead girl and performed a rite for her, he heard the sound of

---

be deciphered. This is a substitute passage borrowed from the text in the Ewha Womans University Collection.

a pipe on the surface of the river. Raising his eyes, he saw a child in green robes approaching on a boat, playing a jade pipe. Yi was about to ask the boy where he should go. The boy said, "If you want to meet Sukhyang, please board my boat."

Pleased, Yi boarded the boat with his mule. The boy stopped playing the pipe and said, "I am the guardian spirit of the river. When Sukhyang fell into the river, we rescued her and sent her on the road. Go in that direction."

Yi gave thanks, then got off the boat and rode his mule in that direction. But all he could see was a dirt field in the distance. No trace of a human. Yi was at a loss when a Buddhist monk appeared, asking, "Where did you come from and where are you going?"

Yi replied that he was lost.

"Go straight until you meet an old man with a horsehair skullcap sitting on a rock. He is Hermit Hwadŏk. If you ask him sincerely where to go, he will tell you. There you will meet the person from your dream."

Yi bade farewell and picked up his pace. Finally he saw an old man with a horsehair skullcap, dozing off, seated on a broad rock under a pine tree. Pleased, Yi approached him and prostrated himself twice. But the old man pretended not to see him. Yi sat on his knees and said, "I'm a wayfarer. May I ask you for directions?"

The old man opened his eyes. "Why do you wake up an old man to talk gibberish? I'm nearly deaf. Speak loudly."

Yi shouted, "I am Yi Sŏn, the son of Duke Yi of Wi in Northern Village in Nagyang. Because I heard that Sukhyang, the daughter of Kim Chŏn in Namyang, is a heaven-sent match for me, I've come a long way to meet her but failed to find her. On my way home I heard you know the answer. Please have mercy on me and tell me where Sukhyang is."

The old man frowned. "I have stayed here for several thousand years and never heard Sukhyang's name or met her. I don't know what crazy monk told you to come to this deep field of eulalia to wake and annoy me with something I have no damn idea about."

Yi prostrated himself again. "It was the guardian spirit of the P'yojin River who told me to come here. Please don't deceive me."

The old man laughed, briefly, but soon grew furious. "I heard that a long time ago a girl fell into the P'yojin River. Maybe the Dragon King of the P'yojin River told you to come here, because he felt sorry for your treating him to ritual food. Anyway, you were deceived."

"It was the Dragon King who told me he saved her and then sent her here."

"Then perhaps she is the one who came here and was burned to death. If you really want to see her, search through the heap of ashes over there and find her charred bones."

Yi searched through an ash pile until he found the ashes of a girl's dress, but no scorched bones. Yi said to the old man, "If Sukhyang died, why can't I find the ashes of her bones, but only traces of her dress?

Please have mercy on me and tell me the truth. Don't lie to me."

The old man dozed off for a long time, then said, "Since you're begging for advice, I'll seek her in my dream. So you must massage the soles of my feet."

Yi obeyed him.

After a long while, the old man woke, sat up, and said, "I traveled the three mountains, ten islands of hermits, four oceans, and eight directions of the world in search of her—in vain. So I asked Lady Hut'o, who said the Old Magu, the Fairy on Mount Ch'ŏnt'ae, took her to the Yihwa Public House in the Eastern Village of Nagyang. When I got there, Sukhyang was embroidering a design on fabric, so I burned the edges of the phoenix's wings on her design. Find the Old Magu the Fairy and ask her where Sukhyang is. If she makes excuses, say, 'Let me see the embroidered phoenix.' If you find burned wings, it's a sign I visited the house."

"The old woman told me to visit Kim Chŏn's house in Namyang. But she wasn't there when I arrived. I had to go a long way to Prime Minister Chang's house before coming here. Tell me the truth. If Sukhyang was at the Yihwa Public House, why did the old woman deceive me?"

The old man laughed. "She's no ordinary person but Grandma Magu the Fairy, who was in charge of affairs on Mount Ch'ŏnt'ae for tens of thousands of years. A heavenly order sent her down to the secular world to take care of Sukhyang. After helping you marry Sukhyang, she'll return to her mountain. She must have deceived you to test your sincerity. No need to make a fuss. But when your parents hear the story, there may be a controversy. Be careful."

Yi rose gratefully again to bid farewell to the old man, but he was already gone. Yi prostrated himself many times to the air and spurred his mule to take him home. His parents were thrilled to see him. "Where have you been for so long?"

Yi lay down on the floor and said, "I met a dear friend."

Sukhyang Ties the Knot with Yi Sŏn

After bidding farewell to Yi Sŏn, the old woman asked Sukhyang, "Did you see the boy?"

"No."

"He's Hermit Prince T'aeŭl, who in his previous life supervised the movements of the stars for the Great Jade Emperor. In this life he's the son of Duke Yi of Wi[75], destined to be your husband. But for his crime in his previous life he has a lump in his eyes, a crooked nose, a nasal polyp, a broken arm, and a crippled leg. He is hideous to look at."

"It wouldn't matter whether he is blind or not if he is Hermit T'aeŭl. How did you know he was T'aeŭl?"

"He told me he followed the Buddha of the Taesŏng Temple to Yoji and received peaches and a cinnamon tree blossom. He also acquired the

---

[75] Two parts of this sentence are missing. This complete translation is based on the text in the Ewha Womans University Collection.

embroidered picture of Yoji that we sold to Cho Chang. Surely he is Hermit T'aeŭl."

"But we don't know everything that are happening in the world. Please check this carefully. If I couldn't find T'aeŭl, I'd rather live alone in my boudoir until I grow old."

"I already thought of that. To test his sincerity, I asked him to search for you in Namyang and Namgun. If he's Hermit T'aeŭl, he'll visit those places and find his way back."

"But you can't count on it. If he really is T'aeŭl, he must have a pearl from my jade ring. I'll keep my chastity until I see it."

"That makes sense." The old woman regarded Sukhyang as praiseworthy.

One day Sukhyang was in a pavilion embroidering the design of a phoenix on fabric, when a flame suddenly rode through the wind to burn the edges of the phoenix's wings. Surprised, she showed this to the old woman.

"That fire came from nowhere. It must be a trick of Hermit Hwadŏk. Someday we'll know the truth," said the old woman.

For three days Yi performed ablutions and purifications in his home. He visited the old woman, carrying the scroll bought from Cho Chang and a thousand *nyang* in gold coins. The old woman saw him in the nick of time and led him to a thatched cottage. They sat down.

She said, "It was not until a couple of days ago that I recovered from my hangover after drinking wine the other day. I haven't tasted any wine since because I have no friends. But now that we meet again, let's get drunk."

Yi prostrated himself twice. "I was given a generous amount of wine the other day. I know I should have paid for it earlier, but I haven't yet. Because I believed your lie, I visited not only Namyang and Namgun but also the P'yojin River and a field of eulalia. I returned home just the day before yesterday. I brought a thousand *nyang* in silver coins. Please accept this small gift as a token of my gratitude."

"I wouldn't decline it, if you insist. But I must tell you that although I live in a poor house I have jars of wine, beneath which is a spring of wine; above are bright stars supervising wine. The jars are always filled with wine. So there is no reason to accept your payment. But you must tell me why you traveled so far."

Yi began to cry. "I went to those places in search of Sukhyang."

"You must be a trustworthy man. To travel a thousand *li* to meet a crippled girl—Sukhyang must be deeply touched to know that."

"She would have been if I had met her. I haven't met her yet. How could she understand?"

She pretended to be surprised. "What? Has she died? Or did she marry someone else?"

"Searching for traces of Sukhyang, I went to the field of eulalia, where I met Hermit Hwadŏk. He said, 'Grandma Magu the Fairy, who lives in the Yihwa Public House in Northern Village in Nagyang, took Sukhyang. When I got there, Sukhyang was embroidering a fabric, so I burned the edge of the phoenix's wings in her design. Go there as soon as possible.' Now here I am in the Yihwa Public House in Eastern Village—the only place with this name. You must have deceived me about Sukhyang."

"You could not have seen Hermit Hwadŏk, because he supervises fire outside the South Gate of Heaven. Grandma Magu the Fairy manages the elixir of eternal life on Mount Ch'ŏnt'ae, so it's ridiculous to claim she came down to earth. To insist that Grandma Magu the Fairy took Sukhyang away is preposterous."

"But Hermit Hwadŏk said, 'If you find the burned wing of an embroidered phoenix, it's a sign that I visited the house.' Please don't deceive me anymore."

"If he really meant it, Sukhyang probably lives here in the Yihwa Public House. But why would I hide her even for a moment knowing that you are desperately trying to find her?"

He was too sad to take a sip of wine. "I'm as good as dead if I can't find her in the three mountains of hermits, the four oceans, and eight directions of the wind." Yi stood up to leave.

The old woman consoled him. "You're Duke Yi's noble son. You can find a beautiful bride and enjoy the spring moon and fall wind any time under mandarin ducks-embroidered blankets and pillows. Why on earth do you seek Sukhyang, who's deformed? I feel bad that you don't understand the torment of your grief."

"I don't hate wealth and honor, nor am I dying for

a bride. I was indifferent to her until I learned who I was in my previous life. Now that I know, I find it difficult even to eat or sleep, thinking of Sukhyang. And when I consider how she was expelled into the world and suffers in her crippled body, how can I not feel for her, though my liver and bowels are made of iron? If I can't meet Sukhyang, I'll kill myself. I can't stay in this world any longer."

"Don't fret too much. They say heaven helps those who help themselves. I'll look everywhere for her."

Yi Sŏn thanked her. "My life depends on you. Have mercy on me." After bidding farewell, he returned home and gazed at the scroll he had bought from Cho Chang, grieving.

* * *

One day, as Yi lingered outside the gate, the old woman rode by on a donkey. He waved to her, inviting her into a detached house. After tidying up the room, he offered her refreshments. "Where are you headed?" he asked.

"There are three girls named Sukhyang. You're free to choose the one you like."

He was delighted. "Where do they live? How old are they?"

"The first girl, eighteen, is the daughter of a royal advisor named Chin Tam. The second, fourteen, is the daughter of Wang Kŏn, minister of defense. The last one, sixteen, was a beggar who doesn't remember her parents. I've notified them all about you; two have responded to my offer. But the damn beggar girl has yet to reply. She said, 'My future husband acquired a pearl from a jade ring at Yoji. I won't surrender my chastity to him unless I see the jewel.'"

Yi was pleased. "The third one must be Wŏlgung Soa. I got the pearl from a fairy who offered me peaches."

He went into the room and returned with a swallow-sized piece of a pearl. "Please give this to the girl and fix a date for our wedding. I'll prepare everything for the ceremony."

The old woman brought the jewel to Sukhyang, who burst into tears at the sight of it. "This pearl is mine. Now everything is at your disposal."

The old woman visited Student Yi the next day. "The girl said the pearl is hers, so I brought her to my house. But why would you marry someone with such an ugly face who is fatally ill? You may believe in your preordained ties and push for the wedding, but it will be difficult for you to look at her every day. She won't be able to marry another man, but will grow old alone feeling bitterness for you. We are in a really awkward situation."

"How can you say such harsh things to me? Sukhyang fell ill because of my sin, not hers. How can I treat her coldly?"

"The girl said, 'I won't marry him unless he follows the proper nuptial rites.'"

"How could I not extend her every courtesy when I accept her as my bride?"

"Do you plan to hold a wedding ceremony after

informing your parents of your marriage?"

"I cannot tell my parents now because they will worry. I'll ask my aunt to prepare for the wedding according to the proprieties."

This was agreeable to her. "Please send gifts to the house of the bride-to-be on the fourteenth day of this month. The wedding will be on the fifteenth."

Yi offered her five hundred *nyang* in gold coins. "Because you're poor, it will be hard for you to come up with the funds for the wedding. Please use this money."

The old woman smiled. "Although I'm poor, I can take care of the costs. You keep these coins to supplement your own living expenses."

Yi Sŏn's aunt, the eldest sister of the Duke of Wi, was the former wife of Yŏ Hŭng, a government official with the senior grade of second rank. Yŏ Hŭng died when she was still childless, and so she loved Sŏn like her own child. When Yi visited her, she said, "I had a strange dream last night, which I was going to ask you about."

"What did you see in your dream?"

"I rode a jade dragon up to Kwanghan Hall, where a fairy told me, 'I will send my beloved Soa to you. Receive her as your daughter-in-law.' I followed the fairy to match you with Soa, and I'm so happy to think you might meet a beautiful bride."

Yi told Lady Yŏ about Sukhyang and the old woman in detail.

She sighed. "Your father's extraordinary character will make it impossible for him to accept a lowly orphan girl as his daughter-in-law. What should we do?"

"I will never marry anyone except Sukhyang even if it costs me my life."

"When you pass the civil service examination and gain a higher position, you will be allowed to have two wives. Your father is doing his service in the capital, so I'll take care of this wedding. Then we can let your father manage your second marriage."

"My aunt, please help me make my dream come true."

"Once your parents hear of this wedding, they will definitely stop it. So wait at your home until the fifteenth, then go to the old woman's house. I'll send abundant gifts to the bride."

Pleased, Yi Sŏn returned home and waited until the fifteenth day of the month.

Lady Yŏ thought, "Sukhyang lives with an old woman, who isn't rich." She prepared opulent gifts to send to the bride's house, then asked her servants: "I heard the bride lives in a commoner's house. How were the household items?"

"We've seen many weddings," they replied. "No other house was so opulent in household items." She was pleased to hear this.

The fifteenth day of the month finally arrived. Yi Sŏn bade farewell to his aunt and went in bridegroom's attire to the old woman's house, where cloud-like shades were drawn and mist-like folding screens put up. The house was decorated with tents and floor mats shining brightly and curtains embroidered with pictures in various colors unseen in the secular world. Yi thought the guests on each side resembled the hermit officers and fairies he had seen in Yoji. When he saw his bride bowing to each side during the ceremony, he found she was the fairy he had seen in Yoji. Delighted, he reaffirmed his love for her, like a couple of mandarin ducks taking a stroll on blue water, like two thrushes perched on a fused pair of trees.

Yi Sŏn came home the next day and met his aunt. Lady Yŏ was pleased. "You told me your bride is crippled," she said. "How is she? I wish to bring her here as soon as possible. Your father doesn't know about her, so please give me notice and bring her to me next time."

"If you wish to see her, look at her portrait in the scroll."

Lady Yŏ said, "She is Soa I saw in my dream." She made plans to persuade the Duke of Wi to bring Sukhyang to his house upon his return from the capital.

Sukhyang's Last Ordeal

Duke Yi was discussing a major border issue with the Emperor. Lady Yi, observing her son's strange behavior, ordered her servants to report what they had witnessed in the house. They told her everything. Surprised, Lady Yi immediately sent word to her husband.

Duke Yi was stunned to learn what happened. "No doubt my eldest sister orchestrated the wedding, and my son must be in love with the bride. So I can't stop him. I heard the girl's an orphan with nowhere to go. I'll let the magistrate of Nagyang secretly dispose of her."

When Yi Sŏn was out to visit his aunt, Sukhyang saw an evening magpie fly into the front window and weep before flying off. She was surprised and worried. "Once a blue magpie came and cried, and I met disaster. What will it cause this time?"

Constables raided her house that night and took her to the magistrate office, where she was forced to kneel.

"I wondered what kind of woman you are, who had seduced the Duke's noble son? The Duke ordered me to put you to death. So don't blame me," the magistrate said. He ordered the constables to bind her arms and legs with ropes and flog her.

"After losing my parents in a rebel uprising in my childhood," Sukhyang said. "I wandered here and there until I settled at the Yihwa Public House. Then the Duke's son proposed to me. As a humble girl relying on an old woman, in a commoner's house, I couldn't dare to resist the offer of a literati family. Thus I became his wife. It's not my fault."

"I know you're innocent. But I can't ignore the Duke's order. I have no choice. Begin flogging her!" The head flogger was about to lash her when he found he couldn't pick up the club, because it was too heavy and his arms ached. The magistrate ordered other floggers to take turns beating her, with the same result.

"This mysterious phenomenon must be the result of trying to kill an innocent person," said the magistrate. "But who will disobey the Duke? Tie her up tight and throw her in the river!"

At that moment the magistrate's wife, Mrs. Kim, dreamed that Sukhyang came to her and said bitterly, "Mother, why don't you help me when Father is about to kill me!"

She awoke and said to her lady-in-waiting, "Where is the magistrate now?"

"He went to the Magistrate's Office," said her lady-in-waiting, "and now he's following Duke Yi's order to execute his daughter-in-law. But for some reason the floggers found it impossible to lash her, so now they are trying to throw her into the river."

Astonished, she ran to the magistrate to plead with him. "More than ten years have passed since we lost Sukhyang, and she never appeared in my dream. But minutes ago she came to me in dream and asked me to save her. Isn't this strange? Why do they want to kill their daughter-in-law? Whose offspring is she? How old is she? And what's her name?"

"Yi Sŏn is the son of Duke Yi of Wi; his gifts are unparalleled in the world. But the Duke's eldest sister secretly orchestrated Yi's wedding. His son abandoned his studies after being enchanted by the girl. Nor can the Duke blame his sister. He couldn't marry his son off to a daughter of a nobleman, so killing the innocent girl is his last resort. I have no choice but to follow the Duke's order, even though I feel pity for her, too."

"If she's the wife of Yi Sŏn, then I want to see her. Don't kill her yet. When you go to the inner yard tomorrow, please give me a chance to meet her."

The magistrate ordered the constables to put her

in jail for the time being.

The girl's fellow inmates felt compassion for her. "You're so beautiful, young bride," they said. "But we're afraid you may die tomorrow."

"Can you tell me what region this is?" she said.

"You're in Nagyang."

Sukhyang decided to inform her husband that she was doomed to die soon. But without brush or ink she was at a loss. When day broke, a blue bird flew onto her lap and cried. She tore off part of her silk jacket, bit her finger, and wrote a letter in blood. When she tied the letter to the bird's leg, it cried twice and flew away.

Yi tossed and turned all night in his aunt's house. His chest felt heavy, and he was distressed for no apparent reason. He went to his aunt's room.

"Have you lost something today?" she said. "Or do you just miss your wife? Why do you wear such a woebegone expression? It's strange. You seem to be losing your mind."

"I've lost nothing in particular. Besides, only one day has passed since I left her. Why would I miss her? I don't know why I'm in distress."

A blue bird flew into the window and perched in front of him. Surprised, Yi found a blood-stained scrap of silk tied to its leg. Yi unfolded the letter:

> *I, Sukhyang, find it hard to pay for my crime in a previous life even in an exile in this world. A tie as strong as metal and stone becomes weak and transient as the blowing wind. A fragrant flower is uselessly turning into soil in a prison in Nagyang. Alas! I will*

die soon without seeing my beloved again. I won't close my eyes even after death.

Yi showed the letter to his aunt, sobbing. He was about to leave for the prison in Nagyang to die with Sukhyang when she said, "Don't act rashly without knowing what's going on!"

She sent one servant to the old woman's house to gather news and ordered another named Wŏnt'ong to go to the magistrate's office and find out what happened.

A former petty official in the provincial town of Nagyang, Wŏnt'ong hurried to the scene and returned to report that the Duke had ordered the magistrate to execute Sukhyang.

Lady Yŏ was furious. "I'll go to the capital to persuade the Duke. If he won't listen to me, I'll go to the palace and tell the Empress everything so that the Emperor will know."

She outfitted herself for the journey and left for the capital that very day, telling Yi, "I'll take care of everything. Don't worry."

Nevertheless Yi took to his bed, wrapping a bandage around his head, determined to die if Sukhyang was killed.

That same day Kim Chŏn went to the office courtyard to summon Sukhyang, whose feeble body was shackled. When she was escorted out by the constables, tears like pearls streamed down her jade-like cheeks. Petty officials and servants looked on in pity, also crying.

"Where were you born?" Kim asked. "What's your

name? Who are your parents? How old are you?"

Sukhyang roused herself. "I lost my parents when I was five and wandered here and there, begging for food. I don't know my hometown or my parents' names. But I heard I was the daughter of a government official named Kim. My name is Sukhyang. Now I'm sixteen."

Tears brimming in her eyes, Mrs. Kim told her husband, "She resembles the daughter we lost. Her name and age are the same as our daughter. She said she's the daughter of an official named Kim, but it's still hard to figure out her family. She looks so pitiful. Please don't kill her. Contact the Duke again to find another way to deal with her."

Kim Chŏn thus sent Sukhyang back to prison, and reported the story to the Duke.

Mrs. Kim missed her lost daughter more and more. "Has she become someone like her somewhere else? Or has she died and turned to dust?" Mrs. Kim wailed loudly.

Mrs. Kim asked her husband to remove Sukhyang's shackles and let her maid servants wash her. Mrs. Kim fed the girl in the prison, consoling her: "Don't worry."

* * *

The letter from Kim Chŏn infuriated Duke Yi, who punished Kim by relegating him to the post of governor of Kyeyang [76] and appointed a new

---

[76] Kyeyang (桂陽), or Guiyang in Chinese, is a city in Hunan

magistrate to execute Sukhyang. Then to his surprise he heard about Lady Yŏ's arrival and went to welcome her.

Lady Yŏ tore into him. "Now that you have a high government post and dignity, how can you think nothing of your parents and sisters?"

Abashed, the Duke kowtowed to her. "I don't understand what you're talking about."

"You govern the country as the Duke. What do you cherish most in human relations?"

"I think the Five Human Relations[77] comes before all else."

"Do you think the five cardinal relations are applicable to relations between you and me?"

"According to propriety, the elder brother should love the younger one, and vice versa. Our relationship, therefore, is surely included in the five relations."

"You hold a high government position, but you're my fifth youngest brother in the family and I stand second to none after our dead parents. But you treat me like a passer-by. Instead of being humiliated, I may as well die here so that you don't need to be bothered."

---

province.

[77] In Confucianism, the Five Human Relationships (五倫) should be governed by *li* (禮), or propriety. Those five basic relationships are between father and son; ruler and subject; husband and wife; older and younger brothers; friend and friend.

Growing pale, the Duke took off his cap, came down to the floor, and apologized. "I'm sorry I don't know my own fault. Please tell me what I have done."

"I raised your son, Sŏn, as my adopted child. He is thus the same as my real son. Days ago, I had a dream, which I told to Sŏn, who told me his own story. He said he may well die without marrying the girl in his dream. I thought, 'If Sŏn passes the state-run civil service examination, he will be allowed to have two wives. This girl is his heaven-sent wife.' That's why I prepared the wedding, which is no different than your own orchestration of a wedding. But now you're going to kill the girl out of resentment. Even though I made a mistake, you should have discussed this with me in private before dealing with it. But now you've deceived me and ordered the Nagyang magistrate to kill the innocent girl in secret. Does that make sense? A man of honor is obliged to govern the world fairly and justly. Why are you going to commit such an outrageous crime that will cause a quarrel in future generations?"

Lady Yŏ's severe rebuke led the Duke to contemplate in silence. "I didn't know you prepared the wedding. A long time ago the King of Yang[78] proposed marriage to our family, which I accepted. But now a controversy has erupted in the royal court over Sŏn marrying a girl of obscure birth. I, therefore, ordered the magistrate to deal with it."

"Conjugal ties are determined by heaven. Love

---

[78] Yang, or Liang (梁) in Chinese, is the name of a country.

doesn't know high or low. In ancient times, a Song dynasty Emperor married a royal concubine after deposing his Empress and loved the girl until death. Of course, the case of Sŏn is different, because I set up the wedding without his parents' knowledge. But if Sŏn passes the state-run examination and gets a high government post, he can have two wives. Then you can choose one girl to be your legal daughter-in-law. Please don't kill an innocent girl."

The Duke was a man of filial piety and loyalty to the nation. He could not defy his eldest sister, although he didn't like her idea very much. "I will obey you, sister."

He called the newly designated magistrate of Nagyang. "Because my eldest sister opposes the idea of killing the girl, I withdraw my order. Don't kill her, but send her to a distant place so that she may not hang around here."

Empress Yŏ, Lady Yŏ's sister-in-law, heard the news of Lady Yŏ's arrival in the capital. The Empress invited her to the palace to stay for over a month. Unable to return to Nagyang immediately, Lady Yŏ sent word to Yi Sŏn that his wife would soon be free. Sŏn was thrilled.

* * *

Duke Yi thought, "As long as Sŏn remains in Nagyang, he will likely bring the girl home."

The Duke ordered a servant to bring his son to

the capital. Yi Sŏn could not hide his sorrows because he had to leave without seeing Sukhyang. Bidding farewell to his mother, Sŏn became tearful.

Lady Yi said, "You married a girl of low birth without your parents' knowledge, and are you reluctant to obey your father's call?"

He told her the story of his marriage. "Sukhyang avoided capital punishment, but she has nowhere to go and no one to rely on without me. Please take pity on her."

The Lady cried. "If she's your heaven-sent wife, who can intervene in your affairs? We don't know what's on your father's mind. Don't worry. Just pass the civil service examination in the capital as soon as possible. Then you can do whatever you want. We won't stop you."

Student Yi wanted to meet the old woman before going to the capital. But the Duke had sent a clear message: "Bring him immediately!" Thus Yi could not disobey the order. After sending a letter to the old woman, Yi left for the capital.

Upon arriving, Yi lay flat before his father. Duke Yi rebuked his son. "Marriage is the most important event in human relations. You were supposed to marry a girl chosen by your parents. You deserve death for marrying a lowly girl without our consent. But I will forgive you this time to save your aunt's reputation. Now you'll go to the National Confucian Academy[79] and study hard. I won't see you outside

---

[79] The National Confucian Academy, or T'aehak (太學) in

the academy until you pass the civil service examination."

Student Yi wept, apologized to his father, and went to the National Confucian Academy. Duke Yi regretted not killing Sukhyang because of Lady Yŏ's intervention.

After Kim Chŏn became governor of Kyeyang, a new magistrate summoned Sukhyang.

He said, "What kind of girl are you to seduce the noble son of an aristocratic family and make him abandon his studies? You deserve death, but I will forgive you this time. After you are released, however, you must go far away."

The magistrate expelled her from the office. The old woman, weeping, was waiting for her at home. She showed Sukhyang a letter from Yi:

> *I, Yi Sŏn, make a deep bow twice to you and send this letter. My shameful heart is beyond expression as you have suffered ordeals both in your previous life and in this world, too—all my fault. Because my father has summoned me to the capital, I must obey the order without seeing you again. Conventional wisdom says that pleasure follows grief and pain follows pleasure. Your painful misfortunes will nearly come to an end, so don't worry too much. I will pass the civil service examination and come back to you as soon as possible.*

Korean, was established in 372, in the second year of King Sosurim's reign in the Goguryŏ Kingdom. The academy taught reading, speaking Chinese, Confucian classics, and martial arts to aristocratic children.

> *You must preserve your precious body no matter what happens. Think that you will enjoy wealth and honor after we reunite in the near future, unburden yourself, having fulfilled your life-long wish of meeting your parents again, dying at the same hour of the day with me before we enjoy everlasting joy. I ardently hope you will cherish your precious life until we meet again.*

Sukhyang wept loudly. "Now that my dear husband has left for the capital and the town office prohibits me from living here, where should I go to find someone to rely on?"

The old woman said, "We'll suffer disaster if you stay here long. We'd better move somewhere else." She demolished the house and moved to another place.

The Old Woman Bids Farewell to Sukhyang

The old woman sighed one day.

"What makes you so sad?" Sukhyang asked.

"It's time to tell you the truth," said the old woman. "I'm Old Magu the Fairy of Mount Ch'ŏnt'ae. I came down to the secular world because Wŏlgung Hang'a ordered me to save you. When you went to the banquet at Yoji, I changed into a blue bird to guide you there. During the wedding ceremony, I invited all the hermit officers of the three auspicious mountains to a sumptuous party. When you were imprisoned in Nagyang, I changed into a blue bird and sent your letter to Yi. Now your ordeals are nearly coming to an end and time is running out for us to live together. That's why I'm so sad."

Sukhyang sank down to the floor and prostrated herself twice to the old woman. "How could a girl ignorant of worldly affairs know you're a fairy? I lost my parents because of my heavy crime in my previous life and finally met you after having suffered indescribable hardships. Because you loved me more dearly than your own child, I thought you might be one of my parents from a previous life. I wished I could repay at least an infinitesimal part of my gratitude to you after I meet my husband again and enjoy happiness. Now that my husband has not come back to me, whom should I rely on when you leave?"

The old woman consoled her. "Our relations are almost finished. This is the will of heaven. Don't grieve. I have long wished to see you enjoy your time with your husband. But how can I resist the heavenly order? The time will soon come when you meet your husband again, enjoy happiness, and reunite with your parents. Don't feel anxious about your future."

"I can't remember my parents' faces and names. How will I know them when we meet?"

"Your father is the local magistrate who almost executed you in Nagyang."

Sukhyang was alarmed. "Why on earth didn't you tell me this earlier?"

"How can I go against the heavenly order when the time is not yet ripe for you to reunite with your parents? But I guided your soul to your mother's dream when the magistrate almost threw you into the river. Then I sat on the arms of the floggers so they couldn't beat you."

"I won't be able to repay your gratitude in this lifetime. But I will in the other world. Now I have nowhere to go. I will have to rely on my parents. Please show me the way."

"Your father is the newly appointed governor of Kyeyang. It would be hard for you to walk three thousand five hundred *li* alone; only with your husband can you go there without difficulty. And if you go there alone you will be fated to part from your husband forever in this life. Now that you have escaped from your bad luck, you can enjoy happiness as well as fortune and glory in the near future. Don't worry. I'll leave this dog with you. Treat it well, as if it was me. It will take care of all your difficulties."

"How far is your destination? And when do you leave?"

"I'll leave soon for Mount Ch'ŏnt'ae, which is more than fifty eight thousand *li* from here."

Dismayed, Sukhyang wept. "I would follow you if it were not so far away. Why don't you stay with me for another day to clear the air?"

The old woman sighed. "Why would I desert you if I could take you there? Your husband will soon come to you, and while I'd like to see him again before leaving I must hurry—time is running out. I'll leave my clothes instead. Clean and shroud my corpse, then prepare a coffin and put my clothes in. Follow the *sapsari* to bury it where the dog digs in the ground, which is my grave. Please visit my grave whenever you face hardship. My spirit will take care of you."

The old woman removed her jacket and laid it on the ground. She took two or three steps. Vanished. Grief-stricken, Sukhyang held the jacket, weeping tears of blood like a mad woman.

Sukhyang folded the clothes, cleaned and dressed the corpse, and put them in the coffin, as the old woman had advised. Sukhyang wanted to follow the dog, which pulled at her skirt and made her sit down. Bewildered, she said to the pallbearers, "The old woman put in her will that she is to be buried where the dog digs in the ground. Please follow it."

They tracked the dog to the west hill in Duke Yi's garden in Northern Village in Nagyang; where it dug in the ground they buried the coffin, so they told Sukhyang upon their return.

Sukhyang cried. "The old woman couldn't forget me even after death. She was buried there in order to watch my husband."

From then on she devotedly performed her rituals morning and evening.

One night she couldn't sleep in the bright moonlight. Nor as she leaned against the window could she overcome her sadness. She wrote down on paper her feelings of loneliness, left the paper on the desk, and dozed off. Waking soon after to find that both the calligraphy and the dog had disappeared, she began to weep.

"Oh, miserable destiny! I have neither anyone to help me nor the dog. How can I spend this fearful, solitary night alone?" She sobbed until she lost consciousness.

***

Yi Sŏn was anxious day and night that news of Sukhyang had stopped since his entry into the National Confucian Academy. One day, with her jade-like face fresh in his memory, he quit his books and loitered in the yard, unable to overcome his sorrow. Then he saw from a distance a creature that resembled a blue lion gazing at him then rushing toward him, crying.

"How strange," he thought. "It looks like her blue *sapsari*. How could it run several hundred *li* to find my residence among all the houses in the capital?"

The animal came closer to him and wagged its tail in delight. It was indeed the dog he saw at the house of Sukhyang. Delighted, Yi patted its head. "You have outperformed me, running a long distance to see me when I dare not go see her."

He was sighing when the dog vomited what appeared to be a letter, which he picked up in alarm. Surely this was her handwriting. He opened the letter:

> *Alas, the ordeal is too harsh for you, Sukhyang. You lost your parents at the age of five and begged everywhere for food for more than ten years, viewed as a person of low status. Why were you falsely charged after staying in another house for more than a decade? How much have you suffered without clearing your tarnished name? Thanks to the gratitude of Old Man*

Wŏlha[80], you met your soul mate and decided to live happily with him for a hundred years. But how were you separated from him even before the bedclothes and pillows were warmed by the heat of love? Because the Ojak Bridge[81] collapsed, you couldn't see each other, and no one will deliver news of each other. You have barely subsisted relying on the old woman. But who will you rely on now that she has passed away? Alas, Sukhyang, this ordeal is too much for you. What bad luck augured this? The world is wide and vast. Why can't you find someplace for your tiny body? Because you may not meet Yi again in your life, you won't close your eyes even after you die.

He thought: "Sukhyang must be thinking of death because she has no one to rely on."

He wept, then fed the blue *sapsari*, hung a letter from its neck, and said, "Now that the old woman is dead, Sukhyang has nowhere to go. You must be the only friend she can rely on. Go back to her as quickly as possible and protect her."

---

[80] Old Man Wŏlha, Yue Xia Laoren (月下老人) in Chinese, is a god who managed the affairs of marriage and love in ancient Chinese mythology.

[81] A legendary bridge formed by a flock of magpies to reunite the lovers—Chingnyŏ, or Zhinü (織女; the Weaver Girl) in Chinese and Kyŏnu, or Niulang (牛郎; the Cowherd) in Chinese for a single day—the seventh day of the seventh lunar month. The collapse of the Ojak Bridge in this context symbolizes the failure of the encounter.

The dog shook its hairy head, kowtowed, and left.

Sukhyang wept as it grew dark. No sign of anyone, nor song of a bird. Exhausted, she clutched her silk handkerchief and lay back against the window, preparing to take her life.

Then she heard a strange sound. Frightened, she stopped weeping and looked outside. A lion-faced creature approached, making the sound of a tree being dragged. She closed the window and hid, but the creature dug its toes into a crack in the door. She recognized it as her *sapsari*. She patted its back. "Where have you been? Why did you leave me alone?"

When the dog lowered its head onto her arm, she found the letter hanging from its neck, which she unfolded with delight:

> *My dear sweetheart! I, Yi Sŏn, made two deep bows to you before writing this letter. You have suffered ordeals both in your previous life and in this world, all because of my crime. What use is there in crying over the past? Since we parted, I haven't sent news because the Galaxy blocks the way and the blue bird hasn't reappeared. I've lost my mind, I'm always anxious, helplessly watching the sun set in the west and the moon rise in the east. Unexpectedly, though, this* **sapsari** *brought me your letter. The sight of your handwriting doubled my joy. But my heart melted when I heard the old woman had passed away. Who will you rely on now? From far away I can feel you spending your days tormented, my heart is like a collapsing mountain. When I look at rice paper and hold my brush, I can't write even one letter, because I feel dizzy, disoriented,*

and cry. They say that pleasure follows grief and pain follows pleasure. Sooner or later the civil service examination will be held; if and when I pass it, with heaven's blessing, I can fulfill my life-long dream of consoling your sad soul. Please take care of your precious body, endure hardships, and wait for me to come back to you. I wish we would die at the same hour of the same day and enjoy our time together after death.

Sukhyang stroked the dog. "The capital is thousands of *li* away from here. How did you get there? If I had known, I would have written a letter detailing the grudges smoldering in my heart. What crime kept me from meeting him when you could go there?" She wept bitterly.

The next day the dog dug in the ground and buried all the household articles it could carry in its mouth. Curious, Sukhyang thought, "The dog is prescient. Something will happen soon." She buried her dresses and dishes in the ground.

Three days later, three or four people approached the house and silently peered into inside. She was curious about their motives, which she could not divine.

After a while, a boy riding a cow said to her, "Those guys will probably rob your house tonight." She asked him why.

"I heard them say, 'She has a lot of treasure in her house. Tonight we'll rob the house, share the treasure, and rape her. We'll make her our woman, too[82].'"

---

[82] This was borrowed from the Ewha Womans University

She was terrified, but could find no way to avoid this. As the sun set, gripped with fear, she warned the dog: "Tonight thieves will rob our house, steal valuables, and rape me. We'd better go to the old woman's grave and die together. Guide me there."

The dog kowtowed. She packed two dresses prepared for her death and left the house. But the dog didn't budge, lying face down on the ground. Only after it was completely dark did the dog rise, bite her bundle of dresses, and drag it along.

"Do you mean we have to abandon this?" she asked.

When she put the bundle down, the dog bit and slung it up on its back. She praised the dog, tied the bundle to its back, and followed it, holding a stick. When the dog came to a garden, she found a grave, and thought: "This must be the old woman's."

She tapped the grave and sobbed. The sound was so sad and desperate it pierced the sky.

Sukhyang's Reunion with Yi Sŏn

In Northern Village in Nagyang, Lady Yi went to the Wanwŏl Pavilion to admire the shining moon. There she heard the wail of resentment and lamentation on the wind at silent midnight[83]. She became curious. "What woman is weeping so sadly in the dead of

---

Collection, because the phrase was erased from the text.
[83] The phrase, "on the wind at silent midnight," was borrowed from the Ewha Womans University Collection, because the original phrase was erased from the text.

night?"

She ordered her servants to look for her. The husband of Student Yi's nanny, standing beside her, volunteered to go. Soon he found a young girl weeping alone. He bowed to her. "Who are you? Why did you come into this garden to weep?"

Afraid of being raped, Sukhyang lowered her head and wept until she realized he was old. Then she told him her story, which so surprised him he prostrated himself. "I'm the husband of Student Yi's nanny. Lady Yi ordered me to find out who was crying. How could I expect it would be you? Please don't stay here in the mountains. Come to my house."

"To meet the husband of Student Yi's nanny is as if I saw my husband. Now I can close my eyes in peace when I die. I don't care if I live or not, because the Duke will try to kill me. But you, too, will be punished for helping me if I go to your house. So I can't follow you."

"You're right. I'll return once I report the situation to the Lady." He ran down the mountain.

The *sapsari* laid the bundle of dresses at her feet, as if to ask her to put them on. She wept.

"If you ask me to wear these dresses, you must be convinced I'll die soon. Please dig in the ground where I'm fated to be buried. After I enter, you can cover my grave with dirt."

The dog did not dig.

"The Duke won't hesitate to kill me once he knows I'm here. This will bring him troubles, too. I'd rather kill myself than be killed by others," she decided, and then tried to hang herself with her silk handkerchief. But the dog bit it off before she died.

"When I asked you to dig my grave, you didn't do it. Now you stop me from killing myself. If you believe I'll see my lover again, step on the old woman's grave, come down, and bow three times. Then I'll follow you, I won't kill myself, I'll believe it's your will that I not die."

The dog went up to the old woman's grave, returned, bowed three times to the grave.

"You're just an animal," she said, weeping, "but you're amazing. I'll follow your will."

The husband went home and told his wife everything about the girl. "She may kill herself while I'm on my way to report this to Lady Yi. Go and protect her."

He went to the Lady and told her the news. Surprised, she said, "Alas, I forgot that!" Then she went to the Duke, and said, "When I gave birth to Sŏn, I recorded the saying of a fairy who helped my delivery. Please read it." She unfolded the note:

The future wife of this baby is Sukhyang, daughter of Kim Chŏn in Namyang.

"What on earth is this?" said the Duke.

"Her name is Sukhyang, and I think she is Sŏn's heaven-sent mate. You should bring her here and listen to what she says about her birth and childhood. You must let Sŏn deal with this when he returns." She ordered ten ladies-in-waiting and a palanquin to bring her.

Sukhyang was weeping when an old woman

prostrated herself before her, saying, "I'm your husband's nanny. My husband just told me that Yi Sŏn's wife has arrived, and I must bring her at once. I'm sorry it took me so long. When I heard that Yi would marry, with Lady Yŏ preparing the wedding, I couldn't see you. I later learned you were imprisoned in Nagyang and then released. But I have since lamented over your loss with my husband because we didn't know your whereabouts."

Sukhyang wept. "You say you're the nanny of my lover. I'm so happy. It's as if I saw him again." When she outlined the story of her hardship, the old woman wailed.

Soon the nanny's husband arrived, carrying a palanquin with ladies-in-waiting, and delivered Lady Yi's message. He asked Sukhyang to climb into the palanquin.

She refused. "Even if the Duke kills me, I will go to the house because disobeying the Lady's order in fear would be the same as disobeying my in-laws. But I dare not ride on the palanquin as a woman of low birth. I'd rather walk."

"But it's the Lady's order. We won't be free of the crime of disobeying her order. Please ride on it," said the old man.

She could not refuse and climbed onto the palanquin, which was filled with fragrance and shone with dazzling lamp and candle-light on either side. Trembling with fear, she arrived at the inner gate of the house, where a lady-in-waiting sent the palanquin-bearers a message from the Lady: "Bring her immediately to the Wanwŏl Pavilion."

The servants set the palanquin down. When Sukhyang followed the light of the candles held by ladies-in-waiting up to the pavilion, she saw the Duke and Lady flanked on both sides by dozens of ladies-in-waiting holding incense and candles that made the room bright as daylight. Sukhyang prostrated herself to them from a distance.

"Come nearer," the Duke and Lady told her.

She stepped forward. The Duke was amazed at her beauty. "She's gorgeous. How could Sŏn not be enchanted by her?"

The Lady cried. "She's so pretty. Conventional wisdom has it that the fairest flowers fade the soonest. She is beautiful even when she's in distress. If she had peace in mind, even Yang T'aejin[84] or Cho Piyŏn[85] would not best her."

"Where do you live? Who are your parents? How old are you?" the Lady asked.

The girl prostrated herself to them and then straightened up. "I lost my parents at the age of five during a bandit riot and then wandered the streets until an animal carried me on its back to Prime

---

[84] Yang T'aejin, or Yang Taizhen (楊太真; 719-756) in Chinese, is better known as Yang Guifei (楊貴妃), the consort of Emperor Xuanzong in the Tang dynasty. She is the supreme paragon of beatuty not only in China but all of Asia.

[85] Cho Piyŏn, or Zhao Feiyan in Chinese (趙飛燕; 32-1 BC), was an empress of Emperor Cheng in the Han dynasty. Her beauty is comparable to that of Yang T'aejin (Yang Taizhen).

Minister Chang's house. Because he and his wife had no children, they raised me as their own child for ten years. I remember neither my hometown nor my parents' names."

"There is only one Prime Minister named Chang Song in Namgun," said the Duke. "Why did you move to the house of the old woman at the Yihwa Public House?"

"A maid servant named Sahyang in the Prime Minister's house slandered me as a thief after she herself stole a golden hairpin from the Lady and put it in a box of my cosmetics. When I was kicked out of the house, I decided to jump into the P'yojin River. Some children plucking lotus flowers saved me and told me to go east. Traveling eastward, I was surrounded by a fire in a field of eulalia. I almost died, and then an old man named Hermit Hwadŏk saved me. The old woman at the Yihwa Public House was passing by and took me to her house."

"How long did it take to go from Prime Minister Chang's house to the Yihwa Public House?"

"I slept in the field of eulalia one night and arrived at the Yihwa Public House the next day."

Duke Yi was shocked. "It's three thousand three hundred and fifty *li* from Prime Minister Chang's house to here. Even if you rode on the fastest horse in the world, it would have been difficult for you to do it that quickly. But you say you made it in less than two days."

Lady Yi asked, "What's your name? In what month and year were you born?"

"My name is Sukhyang. I'm sixteen. I was born

between nine and eleven o'clock at night on the Buddha's birthday, in April of the Year of Kich'uk."

"How can you remember your birth date when you can't recall your parents' names?"

"When I parted from my parents, they tied a small silk bag to a coat string of my dress. When I grew up, I found the hour, date, month, and year of my birth written on soft silk."

Sukhyang untied the pocket and showed it to the Lady, who unfolded it to see Sukhyang's name, the pen name Wŏlgung Sŏn, and the hour, date, month, and year of her birth written in golden letters on a piece of red silk.

Lady Yi was so happy. "You're the same age as my son, and your name is what the fairy told me in a dream. But it's too bad you can't recall your parents' names."

"Since this was written in golden letters, it's quite likely that your father's surname is Kim[86]," said the Prime Minister.

"I heard through the grapevine after I grew up that Kim Chŏn, former magistrate of Nagyang, was my father. But I haven't confirmed that."

"How much better will that be?" The Duke said.

"Can you please tell me who he is?" asked the Lady.

"Kim's the son of Master Unsu, former minister of personnel—one of the noblest families in our country."

---

[86] Kim (金) is both a surname and the word for gold.

"Time will tell us all," the Lady said.

They let Sukhyang stay in the Puyong Pavilion, Yi Sŏn's residence, and when she went into his room, she found a dozen ladies-in-waiting of Yi Sŏn. They served her with sincere respect.

The Lady called on her the next day. "Did you leave anything in your last house?"

"I buried all my dresses and bowls. If thieves haven't stolen them, they will still be there."

"Then tell the servants where to look for them."

"My dog will guide them there."

The Duke, the Lady, and all the servants thought this strange. But the servants followed the dog, unearthed her household articles, and returned with treasures hitherto unseen in the secular world. Then the Duke, the Lady, and all the servants grasped how extraordinary was this girl. From that time on they treated her with special respect.

* * *

One day the Lady asked Sukhyang, "Have you mastered any housework?"

"Because I lost my parents so young and begged everywhere for food, how I could learn anything? But I can do anything once I learn how."

To test Sukhyang's abilities, the Lady gave her a roll of silk. "The Duke's robe, hat and belt are stained, and with my poor eyesight I find it hard to sew. I want you to examine his robe and make a new one. The Duke may have to go to the capital soon."

Returning to her room, Sukhyang found the silk

coarse and of mediocre quality. "How can I make clothes with this?" she thought. "The Lady must be testing my abilities."

She retrieved silk she had already woven and in a couple of days managed to sew a new robe. A lady-in-waiting reported this to the Lady.

"Sewing a robe requires extraordinary skill. I've sewn faster than others since childhood, but it still took me five days to finish a robe working around the clock. How could she do it in two days? Maybe she pretended to sew it." The Lady laughed, calling Sukhyang.

"This is the first robe I've sewn," said Sukhyang, offering it the Lady. "I might not understand the formalities I should follow."

The Lady, astonished, turned pale. "This robe is more than ten times better than the old one in due formalities and sewing skill," she said. "The silk must not be what I gave you."

"That silk was coarse," she said, "so I used silk I wove at the old woman's house. Fortunately, it was the same color as yours."

The Lady praised her before she gave the robe to the Duke, who tried it on. "I haven't worn a proper robe since you grew old," he told her. "This is more exquisite than what I used to wear. I seem to be enjoying the luxury of fine clothes in my old age."

"Sukhyang wove both the silk and the robe with true dexterity."

The Duke was amazed. "She is remarkably skilled."

He awarded Sukhyang a prize, which pleased the Lady.

Presently the Emperor sent a royal secretariat official to the Duke, with orders to come to the capital right away. Dressing for his departure, the Duke looked at his badge of rank. "It doesn't match this gorgeous robe," he said to the Lady. "Can you buy me a new badge?"

"No matter how much you pay, it's hard to buy a badge for this precious robe," she said.

Sukhyang said to the Lady, "What is the design of the Duke's badge?"

"For the first-ranking government official the badge is in the design of a white crane."

"I have a little experience with embroidery. I'll be happy to try, if you give me a chance."

"Embroidering a design for a badge is the most difficult of all. And his departure is imminent. No matter how ambidextrous you are, you couldn't finish it in time."

Sukhyang went to her room. "Embroidering the design for this badge will not be a challenge to me," she thought, and then worked through the night.

The next day, when she gave Duke Yi the badge embroidered with the white crane, he and the Lady were astounded.

"You are indeed a hermit," said the Duke in praise.

When the Duke arrived at the royal palace, the Emperor greeted him with a question: "Where did you get this badge and belt?"

"My daughter-in-law sewed and embroidered them."

"Are you saying your son is dead?"

"No."

"Your robe's design is the wave of the galaxy, and your badge is a crane that lost its mate: a lonely crane standing in the wide sea. If your son is still alive, why did your daughter-in-law sew the design of a lonely woman who lost her husband?"

Alarmed, the Duke lay face down and said, "Your Imperial Highness has the spirit of the sun and moon. Though I have eyes, I didn't recognize my daughter-in-law as a heaven-sent goddess." The Duke then told the whole story of his son's marriage to the girl.

"The fidelity of the woman who embroidered this design will be unparalleled across the ages," the Emperor predicted. "Perhaps heaven sent you this wise woman, because you are the paragon of loyalty and filial piety." The Emperor bestowed upon him many prizes.

The Duke bade him farewell and returned home. He told his family what the Emperor had said and gave the treasures to his daughter-in-law. He and Lady loved Sukhyang more dearly from then on. Everyone in the house respected and admired her with sincerity.

* * *

Yi Sŏn was anxious to meet his bride after sending the *sapsari* away from the National Confucian Academy.

An official at the Royal Observatory reported to

the Emperor, "The Polar Star[87] has reflected the façade of the National Confucian Academy. An extraordinary figure must be studying there."

The Emperor announced a special civil service examination to appoint gifted scholar-officials, who flocked to the capital from across the country.

Yi, too, prepared for the exam and then entered into the examination ground, where the topic for the essay hung from the wall: *On Hearing a Children's Song in a Wide Street*[88].

He unfolded his test paper and meditated on the topic for a while. Then he ground a crimson-colored ink stick on an inkstone engraved with the design of a dragon, dipped a brush made of weasel hair into the ink, and, with a single stroke using the technique of Cho Maengpu and Wang Hŭiji, created a text as energetic as a flying dragon and perfectly complete. Yi submitted the paper to the administrator before any other contestants.

The Emperor read Yi's text and praised it. Every letter deserves a dot of high critical review from the examiners and every phrase a circle for "Excellence[89]." The Emperor chose the winner of

---

[87] In Chinese, the Taiyi Star (太乙星)

[88] This passage, a suggested topic for the examination, symbolized the piping times of peace.

[89] The practice of screening writings in the high civil service examination. Examiners used a dot for writing deserving the highest critical review and a circle for excellence. The Emperor mentioned this because he deemed Yi Sŏn's writing as unparalleled.

the civil service examination, opened the sealed envelope, and checked the name: "The son of Yi Chŏng in Northern Village, Namyang."

The Emperor, quite pleased, told him to ascend to the floor of the Royal Palace. Court guards escorted the exhausted student Yi, who expressed his gratitude lying face down.

The Emperor found his face was the color of jade decorating the crown, his posture like that of Tu Mokchi. The spirit of mountains and rivers gathered at the midpoint of his eyebrows and the harmony of heaven and earth was embodied in his heart. The vital force gleamed in his eyes, as if reflecting the Big Dipper and the Herdsman. His gift was unmatched even by Kang T'aegong[90] of Chu, Chang Chabang and Che Kallyang[91] of Han.

The Emperor poured three drinks in succession for Yi and ordered to perform band music to be played at court. He awarded Yi the paper flower given to the top prize winner, gave him the finest mule to ride home, and appointed him a scholar in the Office of Royal Documents. Expressing his

---

[90] Kang T'aegong, or Jiang Taigong (姜太公) in Chinese, is a popular name for Jiang Ziya, an 11th-century BC statesman. He is the most famous angler in the history of China.

[91] Che Kallyang, or Zhuge Liang (諸葛亮; 181–234) in Chinese, was the most acclaimed strategist during the Three Kingdoms period in old China. Often compared to the Chinese strategist Sun Zi, Zhuge Liang appears in a 14th-century historical novel *Romance of the Three Kingdoms* by Luo Guanzhong.

gratitude, Yi made a deep bow to the Emperor and left. He escorted Lady Yŏ on the way back from the capital, with band music playing; residents and passers-by in the capital jammed the street in order to watch him.

Entering Nagyang, Yi told Lady Yŏ, "I owe my success on the examination with honors to the Buddha at the Taesŏng Temple. So I must express my gratitude to the Buddha first. Would you please prepare something for the party?" Lady Yŏ agreed, allowing him to go on ahead.

Yi went to the Taesŏng Temple to pay his respects to the Buddha. He arrived at the Yihwa Public House, which had fallen into ruin. He began to cry. "Because my love suffered hardship instead of me and died, what good is passing the civil service examination? I'll go to her grave after seeing my parents and die there."

When he got home, the Duke and Lady went out to the inner gate to greet him as the winner of the civil service examination.

The Duke, seeing that Sŏn was unhappy, said, "You passed the civil service examination at such a young age and brought honor to our family. You should be happy. But your face is lined with tears. What worries you?" Sŏn sighed, gazing at the sky in silence.

Lady Yi recognized what was in his mind. "Do you think your wife is dead? We brought her to our house long ago. So stop worrying."

Sŏn couldn't believe what his mother said. "I'm tired, I drank too much on the long journey home."

Without removing his robe, he leaned against the banisters and lay down.

The Lady ordered her lady-in-waiting to bring in the bride.

Sukhyang appeared, weeping, and held fast to the sleeve of Yi's robe. Yi couldn't tell if he was awake or dreaming, crazy or drunk. Terrified, he held her delicate hands and wept.

Sukhyang calmly said, "You must be tired from your journey. You should get some sleep."

Yi recovered his senses at the sound of her voice and looked around, recognizing he was in his own house. Everyone—ladies-in-waiting, servants standing in line, his relatives—consoled him. He thanked his wife. "Lucky I passed the civil service examination, but my anxiety over you almost melted my heart. I visited the Yihwa Public House on my way home, but heard no birdsong and found no trace of anyone—which melted my heart. Now that I see you again, what more could I wish for?" He wept and wept.

People said, "Their preordained tie is so close. How could the Prime Minister stop them?"

When Yi asked Sukhyang what hardship she had suffered, she sighed. "Today is a happy day for us. I don't feel like telling you my story now. I'll tell it to you in the distant future."

She helped him change his robe. Then he went into the room and greeted his parents. They were very happy. The Duke threw parties for three days to celebrate his son's success in the civil service examination, followed by another three-day festivity at Lady Yŏ's house. Relatives, close or distant, and villagers—all celebrated Sŏn's victory.

One day the Duke called Sŏn. "I've watched Sukhyang in my house and found her conduct and propriety are sincere and immaculate. Because you married her secretly, though, people will talk behind your back. Long ago, I accepted the King of Yang's proposal of marriage. Now he will want the wedding to take place. What shall we do?"

"That can be easily settled. Don't worry. I'll take care of it," Sŏn said.

He left for the capital, met the Emperor, and told him the story of his relation to Sukhyang. The Emperor had already heard her story. After listening to Yi Sŏn, the Emperor told government officials, "Sukhyang's propriety is unparalleled even by those from the past, so I will designate her as the Lady of High Virtue and Chastity."

The minister of personnel matters said, "It is the custom of our country that a wife's title of nobility be decided according to her husband's. Yi ranks fifth in terms of the degree of nobility, so it is against the rule to offer his wife the first rank."

"Do you mean a woman of propriety can't accept a high government post if she lives without a husband?" the Emperor asked.

The Emperor gave a special order for Yi to take the government post as a royal advisor and his wife to be the Lady of High Virtue and Chastity. Government ministers were perplexed by this order but dared not defy the royal order. Yi gained more fame, and he also held the posts of manager of documents and royal advisor, respected by everyone at court.

When the King of Yang sent someone to arrange the wedding, the Duke didn't know what to do. But Yi said, "I'll nullify the agreement. Don't worry about it[92]."

Sukhyang Revisits Prime Minister Chang's House

The people of Hyŏngch'o had several years of bad harvest and plundering, which worried the Emperor. Yi Sŏn stepped forward.

"The will of heaven may change according to the hearts of the people," he told the Emperor. "Because public officials in Hyŏngch'o failed to take care of the people, the region has suffered many natural calamities. And those who were cold and starving turned into robbers and rose up in rebellion. I have no special talents, but I can console the people and stop the thieves if I am given a chance to reign over the region."

The Emperor was happy to appoint him inspector-general[93] of Hyŏngju. "Go rule the land

---

[92] Part of this paragraph is missing or is undecipherable. Thus "The Duke didn't know what to do, so Yi said" is borrowed from the text in the Ewha Womans University Collection.

[93] This position, created in the Han dynasty, persisted through the Tang and Song dynasties until it was abolished in the Ming dynasty.

of Hyŏngch'o," he said. "Check out the country governors and local magistrates and fire or retain them at your own discretion."

Yi expressed his gratitude, went home, and told his father about his mission to Hyŏngch'o.

The Duke said, "They say a man of courage has few days to serve his parents but many days to serve the Emperor. There is no regret in going to gain honor. But Hyŏngch'o is one thousand *li* away from here, and the region is crowded with thieves. I'm so worried."

The new inspector-general said, "I'm going there to protect the people and to invalidate the King of Yang's proposal of marriage. Don't worry."

He told the Lady of High Virtue and Chastity, "I'll go there first. You can follow later."

"How far is Namgun from Hyŏngch'o?"

"Namgun is part of Hyŏngch'o, so I'll visit the town on my way to Hyŏngch'o."

"I'll visit several places on my way to offer gratitude. Will that be all right?"

"Do whatever you like."

He bade farewell to his parents and left for Hyŏngch'o. The thieves grew anxious when they learned Yi was the new inspector-general. "Will he execute us all at once?" they wondered.

Upon arriving in Hyŏngch'o, Yi Sŏn went on patrol, dismissing or promoting officials according to their skills or misdeeds. He encouraged people to devote themselves to farming, evenly distributing grain from the warehouses. Thieves became good citizens. People lived comfortably. Yi calmed the public, and his praises were sung far and wide.

The Duke, returning from the capital, called Sukhyang. "I heard your husband has turned the thieves of Hyŏngch'o into good citizens. Hyŏngch'o is no longer dangerous, so he's waiting for you. It's time to prepare for your journey to Hyŏngch'o."

Sukhyang ordered her ladies-in-waiting to prepare sacrifice for the graveside ritual. She performed ritual for the old woman, after which she fed her *sapsari*[94]. Sukhyang patted it, cooing, "My *sapsari*! If not for you, I would be dead and turned to dust."

While she grieved, the dog pawed the ground, whimpering. Sukhyang read a sentence scratched in the dirt: "Our relationship has ended, so I must leave you."

She was taken aback. "After so much suffering, I have become the Lady of High Virtue and was about to repay my gratitude to you. But since you're leaving me, I can't endure this sorrow. Do you have to go now?"

The dog pointed its nose at the old woman's grave, prostrated itself to Sukhyang, and took three or four steps before roaring. It then disappeared in a dark cloud.

Sukhyang's eyes brimmed with tears. "Even a dog sent down from heaven has suffered for me." She buried the dresses where the dog disappeared and

---

[94] Part of the sentence was erased—"to prepare sacrifice for the graveside ritual. She performed ritual for the old woman, after which she fed her *sapsari*"—was borrowed from the text in the Ewha Womans University Collection.

performed a ritual for it.

She bade farewell to the Duke and Lady and left the house, telling the servants, "I have to perform rituals in several places on my way to Hyŏngch'o. Prepare sacrificial offering properly and tell me the name of each town we pass."

When they came to the field of eulalia, Sukhyang remembered Hermit Hwadŏk's gratitude, wrote a ritual ode and then performed a rite, after which she discovered that the wine in the glass had evaporated, leaving behind a goose egg-sized bead. This mysterious bead she tucked into her blouse before leaving the field.

They arrived at a river. Sukhyang asked the servants, "Is this the P'yojin River?"

"It's linked to the P'yojin River, which is a thousand *li* away by ship. This is the Yangjin River."

"You mean we can get there by water?"

"Yes, but the route is dangerous. They usually cross the river and go by land." Sukhyang was disappointed to hear that.

They were halfway across the river when the east wind rose so fiercely the ferryman lost his oars. The wind blew harder yet, the waves soared into the sky, and the boat was swept westward fast as a flying arrow. The people in the boat lost their minds, thinking death was imminent. The wind died down after a while and the waves subsided. When night fell, they grew hungry. Because this vessel was for official use, it had no burners or caldrons. They searched in vain for food along the riverbank. They felt bewildered and embarrassed.

They heard the sound of piping on the water and were about to ask the pipers the way[95]. The boat flew by as if on the air. Two fairies stopped piping to recite a poem.

> *We met the girl Sukhyang here on this same day last year.*
> *Today we encounter her again as a Lady.*
> *Our delight is more than ten times greater,*
> *but we can't tell her truth because of others surrounding her.*
> *Where can we find the bead of Hermit Hwadŏk*
> *and feed the hungry passengers?*

She could see their faces and hear their voices clearly. But her ladies-in-waiting and the others in the boat heard only piping sound. She thought: "Maybe the bead I found at the ritual site for Hermit Hwadŏk is the mysterious bead I can use for boiling rice."

She ordered her ladies-in-waiting to wash rice and put it in a big bowl. When she added the bead, the rice came to a boil. The passengers praised her. "Our Lady is herself a hermit."

Presently the boat arrived at the P'yojin River.

---

[95] The following is the text from the Ewha Womans University Collection, which tells the circumstances more precisely: "She heard the sound of piping on the water. When she looked out through the bead curtains, she saw two fairies piping on an approaching lotus flower boat. On closer inspection, she found they resembled the fairies who had saved her in the Pyojin River. Delighted, the Lady was about to ask them the way."

Alarmed, the boatman said, "The Yangjin River is one thousand nine hundred *li* from here. Even with a fair wind, we couldn't have sailed here so fast. The way is so dangerous, only one out of a hundred vessels ever reaches this river. We left at dawn and arrived in the afternoon. I've never had such a strange experience."

The Lady was preparing sacrificial offerings to perform a ritual for the Dragon King, when five-colored clouds rose from the water to encircle the boat. When the clouds cleared, they saw that all the ritual foods were gone and the bowls were filled with gold and silver. A duck egg-sized bead produced a glittering light in the wine glass.

Sukhyang thought: "Surely the wife of the Dragon King ate the ritual food." She collected all the treasures and got ashore.

* * *

A servant said to Sukhyang, "Now we're in Namgun, in the land of Hyŏngju[96]. I suggest we find quarters here."

"I heard the house of Prime Minister Chang is not far away. Where is it?"

"The hill before us is his property."

"I'm too tired to walk any further. Tell the magistrate to prepare all the formalities[97] for progress.

---

[96] Hyŏngju, or Jingzhou (荆州) in Chinese, is the province where Hyŏngch'o (荆楚) is located.

[97] These formalities include attire, palanquins, and escorting

We'll stay tonight in the house of Prime Minister Chang."

A servant sent her message to Han Pok, governor of Namgun, who was surprised to learn of the Lady of High Virtue and Chastity's arrival. He prepared formalities and hastened to Prime Minister Chang's house. When the Lady's company arrived, three thousand nimble soldiers adorned in five-colored suits of armor and two dozen ladies-in-waiting decorated with seven treasures and holding incense and candles were lined up on both sides of the parade. To the accompaniment of band music, the Lady entered the mansion riding on a golden palanquin.

It was spring. Alarmed at hearing of the Lady's arrival, Prime Minister Chang ordered servants to lay out a silk carpet before the Yŏngch'un Pavilion to greet her parade. All of Namgun grew boisterous. A large number of people gathered to see the rare parade.

Lady Chang sent Sukhyang her greetings through a lady-in-waiting named Ch'unhong:

> *Your noble presence is visiting our humble house—a splendor for us. I know I must greet you straightaway. But I'm afraid I can't meet you now because I am scheduled to perform a ritual for the dead tonight. Please allow me to come and meet you tomorrow, if you don't mind.*

---

guards for senior officials.

Sukhyang sent this letter in reply:

I was fortunate enough to appreciate the scenery in this wonderful land as our company passed by. I am deeply grateful for your hospitality of sending me kind greetings in advance. I assume no strict etiquette is needed between housewives. I will pay you a visit tomorrow.

Ch'unhong brought Sukhyang's message to Lady Chang.

"How elegant was the Lady of High Virtue and Chastity?" Lady Chang asked.

"She was attended by many ladies-in-waiting through whom she sent her message to me. I couldn't see her, so can't tell you about her countenance. But all the ladies-in-waiting recited a poem she wrote at the Yŏngch'un Pavilion. She must be a gifted writer."

"Can you recite it for me?"

Ch'unhong recited the poem:

When I greeted spring in the Yŏngch'un Pavilion last year,
  the flowers on the stone steps laughed at me for my tardy admiration.
When I greet spring again in the Yŏngch'un Pavilion this year,
  the flowers smile at me to celebrate our reunion.
They smile, overwhelmed with delights,
  but I feel sad at the renewed thought of the past.

There was something unusual about the poem,

Lady Chang thought, and said so to her husband. He said, "That's so strange. The Lady of High Virtue and Chastity—a newcomer to the Yŏngch'un Pavilion—wrote this poem as if she had been here before. I can't understand its real meaning. But she is certainly a gifted poet." He wrote the poem down on paper.

Sukhyang talked late into the night with her lady-in-waiting then went to sleep. In dream she entered Lady Chang's room and saw her portrait hanging from the wall and a feast spread on the table. Lady Chang wept before the portrait. "Sukhyang! If you had lived, you would have married into a noble family and become a woman like the inspector-general's wife."

Sukhyang woke up and realized it was only a dream.

"Lady Chang and I must have a powerful tie," she thought. "Years ago, I fell into the P'yojin River after Sahyang's slander got me kicked out of the house. But now the Lady is performing a memorial service for me." Lady Chang's devotion and sorrow impressed her.

The next morning, Sukhyang outfitted herself magnificently to greet Lady Chang.

"I'm the Prime Minister's wife," said Lady Chang, "but I've never seen such gorgeous attire. It's my great honor to see such a precious spectacle."

Lady Chang hosted a banquet, with the same dishes prepared that Sukhyang had seen in her dream the night before. Sukhyang was impressed.

"I couldn't go to the governor's office," she said,

"exhausted as I was from traveling. While looking for a place to rest, my servants guided us to your house, where I watched a spectacular scene and was heartily greeted by you. I was deeply moved by your hospitality."

"May I ask how old you are?" Lady Chang asked.

"Twenty."

Lady Chang began to cry.

Sukhyang was taken aback. "What makes you so sad?"

"Because of our crimes in a previous life," she said, "my husband and I were childless. But later we met a girl and raised her as our foster child until she died five years ago. Last night marked the fifth anniversary of her death. So I performed a ritual for her. She was the same age as you, which made me think, 'If she had lived, she would be a lady like you.'"

A magpie flew into the banister just before she finished speaking, and cried. "Sukhyang died an innocent death after you cried here," said Sukhyang. "Why do you come here again?"

"How do you know so much about Sukhyang without having been here?" said Lady Chang.

"I once bought an embroidered scroll titled 'Sukhyang,' and came to know her story."

"Have you by chance brought the scroll with you?"

Sukhyang asked her lady-in-waiting to fetch it. Here was her personal history in chronological order: *A deer carried Sukhyang to the garden of Prime Minister Chang; the Prime Minister saw Sukhyang dozing in a bush and called his wife; Lady Chang raised Sukhyang like her own daughter; Sukhyang worried after seeing a magpie cry on the day of the party at the Yŏngch'un Pavilion; Sukhyang tried to kill herself in front of Lady Chang after Sahyang slandered her; Sukhyang wrote a letter with blood in her room*[98]*; Sahyang rebuked Sukhyang and kicked her out of the house; and Sukhyang plunged into the river.*

Gazing at the picture, Lady Chang recalled the scenes as if they had happened just a day ago and began to cry. Sorrow came over Sukhyang.

"I've seen this picture so many times that I knew about the Yŏngch'un Pavilion. I mentioned the magpie because it came and cried again. I'm sorry for your sorrow."

Lady Chang wept for a while before speaking. "The scroll reveals everything that happened in our house. What else can we hide from you?" She told Sukhyang every detail: how she raised Sukhyang as her favorite child; how Sahyang was struck dead by lightning for slandering Sukhyang; how she sent servants to search for Sukhyang in the P'yojin River; and how the Prime Minister bought this portrait of Sukhyang because she was so distraught.

"Parents generally forget their own children a year after they die. But how is it that you can't forget the child of others for such a long time?" Sukhyang asked.

"If I can't meet Sukhyang in the next world, let alone this one, my yearning for her will not end even after ten million years. But it is as if I saw Sukhyang again in this once-in-a-lifetime chance to see your

---

[98] Part of the text is missing—"in her room" comes from the text in the Sim B Collection.

scroll. Now I can close my eyes when I die. Please sell me the painting."

"I wish I could give it to you for free. But my husband loves it, and he paid double for it. I can't just give it to you. But if you'll pay me well, I'll sell it to you."

"I live in a poor house, so I can't pay much. But I had ten thousand *nyang* in gold coins and three thousand servants to give to Sukhyang when she grew up. I don't need them now that she's dead. I'll give them all to you. Please sell it to us."

"You said you have the portrait of Sukhyang. I want to see it."

"It's hanging in my bedroom."

Sukhyang followed Lady Chang into the room, where the portrait hung from the wall around which silk curtains were drawn. A feast was set on the table. She stepped forward.

"You couldn't forget Sukhyang because you couldn't forget her face in the portrait. I know I'm not that pretty, but could you compare me to her?" Sukhyang removed her ceremonial coronet and adjusted herself like a girl. Drawing open the silk curtains, she stood beside the portrait. Everyone was shocked.

"Either the portrait of Sukhyang has turned into the Lady of High Virtue and Chastity, or vice versa!" they said. Ecstatic and bewildered, Lady Chang burst into tears.

Sukhyang prostrated herself.

"How could I have known you were still thinking of me?" She pointed to her old bedroom. "I'm

Sukhyang. Can you see my letters written in blood?"

Lady Chang fainted. When she woke up, she hugged Sukhyang and stamped her feet.

"My daughter, I thought you were dead. How could I imagine you would return to me as a noble person?" She wailed.

Prime Minister Chang rushed to the scene and embraced Sukhyang. He wept loudly.

"Don't weep," Sukhyang said. "I've come to celebrate our reunion. Enjoy yourselves."

She ordered her ladies-in-waiting to bring proper attire for Prime Minister and Lady Chang; prepared food for three days of banqueting; invited all the housewives in the neighborhood.

"The Prime Minister used to complain about not having a child. But now he is happier than those who have children." Everyone praised Sukhyang.

After a month in the Prime Minister's house, Sukhyang bade farewell to them.

"Hyŏngju is not far from here. My husband, the inspector-general, will send his servants to you. Please come and visit us."

Prime Minister and Lady Chang agreed.

Sukhyang gave many treasures to Prime Minister and Lady Chang. Despite their joy, they grieved at the prospect of her departure.

Sukhyang's company left Namgun and arrived in Changsa, where red and blue birds as well as storks and cranes flocked together in the mountains. The birds were not afraid of people. The servants fired arrows at them until Sukhyang stopped them.

"Don't hurt the animals." Sukhyang sent a

message to the government office in Changsa, ordering them to bring ten sacks of rice there. Her servants boiled the rice. At the entrance to the valley, she said to the birds, "Eat this steamed rice. You rescued me in the past."

Instantly the birds flocked together and pecked at the boiled rice before flying away. Again and again, they looked back at her.

"I've repaid my debt to you all," she told herself, "but I still haven't met my parents. When can I repay my gratitude to them?"

They arrived in what a servant said was the town of Kyeyang. Sukhyang was pleased. "When the old woman died, she told me my father was Kim Chŏn, governor of Kyeyang. I'll see my parents soon." She grew anxious.

The governor of Kyeyang came to greet Sukhyang, offering his name plate: *Yu To, governor of Kyeyang*.

Surprised, Sukhyang asked her servant, "I thought the governor was Kim Chŏn. Why is this governor's name different? Is there another Kyeyang under heaven?"

"Kim Chŏn was governor not long ago. But the new inspector-general appointed him governor of Yangyang[99] in recognition of his wise ruling. Yu has succeeded Kim."

Sukhyang was disappointed. "How far is Yangyang from here?"

---

[99] Yangyang, or Xiangyang (襄阳) in Chinese, is a city in Hubei Province in China.

"About three hundred *li*."
"We'll stop by Yangyang on our way to Hyŏngju."
"Then we will have to make a long detour."
Sukhyang nevertheless wanted to go there. But if her company don't take a direct route, it would be a burden on her servants and the townspeople; it would also make her a target of public criticism. She was in an awkward situation.

Sukhyang Reunites with Her Parents

Kim Chŏn was relegated to the governorship of Kyeyang as punishment for failing to execute Duke Yi's daughter-in-law. Yi Sŏn inspected government offices, promoted governors or local magistrates to higher posts or dismissed them depending on their performance. Yi found that Governor Kim Chŏn administered public affairs properly and was admired by the people. Yi promoted him to governor of Yangyang, which was about the same size as Hyŏngju.

One day Kim Chŏn was on his way home from visiting the inspector-general of Hyŏngju. He arrived at the Pan River, where an old man[100] seated on a rock didn't move when Kim's company passed. Kim's servants tried to arrest him. Noticing something unusual about the old man, Kim ordered

---

[100] Half of the line in the original text is missing—the phrase "arrived at the Pan River, where an old man" is borrowed from the text in the Ewha Womans University Collection.

the servants to step back. He dismounted his horse, approached the old man, and bowed to him. The old man pretended not to see him, which Kim found curious.

"An ordinary man would be afraid of someone accompanied by three thousand armored cavalry soldiers," Kim thought. "But he grows more arrogant. Strange." Kim made another bow. The old man ignored him, crossed his legs, lay back, resting his head on one arm.

"You may go your own way. I don't think I asked you to bow to me," the old man said.

"I bowed to you out of respect, since you are older than me."

"If you truly respected your elders, you would have left me alone after bowing in the distance. But you were thinking, 'I got a higher government position thanks to my son-in-law.' You approached me without my permission. What do you want to ask me?"

"I just expressed my respect to an elder. But you abused me instead of being pleased. You said my incumbent position is indebted to my son-in-law, who doesn't exist. I have no child."

The old man was infuriated. "If you have no child, where did Sukhyang come from? Did she fall from heaven or spring up from the earth? Was she pressed out of a hole in a rock or begotten by a hairy beast? Who on earth gave birth to Sukhyang if you don't know her?"

Alarmed, Kim made two deep bows to the old man. He lay flat on the ground, pressing his face into the earth. "I'm a miserable person," he said, "who can't see the truth because I only have eyes without eyeballs. I'm sorry I was rude to you. Please forgive me."

The old man brightened.

Kim drew himself up on his knees. "Because I committed a serious crime in my previous life, I was childless until I got a daughter in my old age. Her name is Sukhyang, her pen name is Wŏlgung Sŏn, and when she was five a riot broke out. We hid her between rocks on Mount Panya, but never found her again. We thought she must have died and gave up searching for her. Please tell me her whereabouts, if you know it."

"I heard stories of her survival or demise. But I can't speak now because I'm very hungry."

Kim ordered his servant to get wine and food from a tavern[101]. The old man was outraged.

"If you give me food bought by your servant, it will be no more than his effort. Do you mean I have to tell you the whereabouts of your servant's daughter?"

Kim rushed to the tavern himself, where he sold his horse to buy boiled pork and a hundred bottles of fine wine. The old man polished them off in no time.

"I'm drunk, so it's hard to speak now. If you want to know Sukhyang's whereabouts, dismiss your

---

[101] Part of the text is missing. The phrase "to get wine and food from a tavern" is borrowed from the text in the Ewha Womans University Collection.

servants and wait until I sober up." He closed his eyes and fell asleep, snoring loud as thunder.

Kim ordered his servants and soldiers to wait at the tavern. He stood by the old man politely, with his arms folded. Suddenly it grew dark, a heavy shower poured down, and the water rose up to his shoulders. Kim didn't move until it stopped. Then a cold wind rose and snow piled up to his shoulders. Kim found it hard to stay awake in the cold. But he didn't move, though his clothes had frozen. He was shivering so hard he couldn't speak.

The old man awoke and sat up. He laughed. "I made you suffer in order to examine your conduct. I'm impressed by your sincerity."

The old man removed a red fan from his sleeve and waved it, melting the one-*kil*[102]-high snow. The weather grew warm as summer again.

Kim realized how extraordinary the old man was and twice made a deep bow. "Please tell me where Sukhyang is."

"If I tell you her itineraries, will you visit all the places she went?"

Kim twice made a deep bow to him. "I'll find her wherever she is, only if you tell me."

"After you hid her between the rocks, bandits took her."

"Is she living in the camp of the bandits?"

"They brought her to a remote mountain village. Guided by a phoenix, she visited the palace of Lady Hut'o. Are you willing to go there?"

---

[102] One *kil* equals approximately 2.4 to 3 meters.

"Has she died?"

"Lady Hut'o ordered a deer to take her on its back to the house of Prime Minister Chang. She was reportedly raised as a foster child of Prime Minister and Lady Chang, who were childless. You may meet her there."

"Shall I go tomorrow[103]?"

"But the infernal maid servant Sahyang wrongfully accused her and kicked her out of the house. Sukhyang plunged into the P'yojin River and visited the underwater palace of the Dragon King. You may find her there."

"If she lives on earth, I may find her body. How can I search for her underwater?"

"Some children picking lotus flowers in the Jade River gave her a ride on a lotus leaf boat and dropped her off on the northbound road. She took a wrong turn and met a grass fire on the field where she was sleeping. They say she was burned to death. If you go there, you may find the ashes of her bones. Go and seek them."

"If she died there, how can I find her ashes?"

"She almost died in the fire. But Hermit Hwadŏk rescued her and took her to Magu the Fairy. If you search ardently for her in the human world, it might be possible to find her."

"Where can I find her in this wide, wide world?"

The old man looked him in the eye. "Why are you so desperate to find her?"

---

[103] This sentence is missing. This is from a text in the Ewha Womans University Collection.

"I gained a daughter in my later years. But I lost her thanks to my lack of affection for her. I felt as if heaven fell to earth, and cry now day and night. But heaven helped me and sent me a saint today. I'll pray for you ten million times and more. Please help me find Sukhyang."

The old man grew infuriated again.

"Then why did you desert her on Mount Panya? Why did you try to kill her on someone's order without trying to meet her when she was imprisoned in Nagyang? Now you desperately seek her! You badger an old man to find her, like a child pestering his father for something."

Kim prostrated himself twice again. "My wife and I had to leave her on Mount Panya, because we were about to be killed in a riot. The girl put behind bars in Nagyang was named Sukhyang and was the same age as my daughter. But I didn't double-check because I wasn't certain. Every disaster has resulted from my lack of generosity. Please tell me. If you do, I'll repay my gratitude as if I were your son." Kim was begging.

The old man laughed. "It's not your fault. Everything was predestined by heaven. I'm the Dragon King who protects this river. A long time ago, my child was turned into a turtle and almost died when she was caught in a fisherman's net cast into the Pan River. You saved her, so I came here to repay my gratitude. I asked the Great Jade Emperor for a way to find her. If not for your sincerity, I wouldn't have told you the truth."

The old man continued. "Listen carefully.

Sukhyang has suffered five near-death experiences, and she has become a noble presence. Hence you'll find her sooner or later. Because you didn't know about her hardships, you wouldn't recognize her even if you meet her. Thus when you do meet her, ask her all the questions I spelled out for you. If she relates the same experiences, you can confirm that she's your daughter."

Kim expressed his gratitude. "Even if I meet my daughter, we'll have no way of recognizing each other after so many years. I'm grateful to you, Dragon King, for telling me her story. May I ask you something else? Is Sukhyang the wife of the inspector-general? Please tell me."

"Time will tell you everything. We will meet again." Then he vanished.

Kim returned home with his security guards. When he told his wife what the Dragon King had said, she prayed to heaven. "I would have no regrets if I died now, if only I could meet her again. But if she has become the inspector-general's wife, how would we dare call her our daughter?" She was overcome with sorrow.

***

Sukhyang was in an awkward situation, because she couldn't go to Yangyang. Nor could she sleep under the bright moon. She leaned against the window, sighing. "Perhaps my parents are gazing at the same moon. But how will they know how sorry I am gazing at it?"

Unable to resist her sorrow, she wandered around her room, weeping. Suddenly a fairy came down from the clouds.

"It's been a long time! How have you been getting along since we parted?"

Sukhyang was startled. "I'm sorry I can't recognize you in the dark."

"Perhaps you've already forgotten me. I'm the Old Magu the Fairy on Mount Ch'ŏnt'ae. On my way to meet Yŏ Tongbin, Chŏk Songja[104], and Yi Chŏksŏn, I dropped by to let you know that if you want to meet your parents, you should go to Hyŏngch'o. You'll meet them within some months." She disappeared.

"The old woman told me the way. She didn't forget me. I'll go to Hyŏngch'o and meet my parents, even if I would be criticized." Sukhyang wept.

The next day she ordered her servants to notify the administration office of Yangyang of her impending arrival. In each town she visited along the way, she invited the wives of the local magistrates to get together to talk. The company finally arrived in Yangyang.

Hearing of her arrival, Kim Chŏn said to his wife, "The Lady should have gone first to Yangyang if she was planning to leave the capital for Hyŏngju. It's strange that she has already passed Namgun and made a detour in Kyeyang before coming here. The

---

[104] Chŏk Songja, or Chi Songzi (赤松子; Master Red Pine) in Chinese, is a Chinese rain god.

other day, the Dragon King of the Pan River said that Sukhyang will come back as the inspector-general's wife. I think Sukhyang will visit us."

Mrs. Kim sighed. "I had a mysterious dream last night, so I thought I would hear some good news. I myself will inquire her background."

She ordered a servant to check the lady's history. Kim and his wife were disappointed to hear that she was the daughter of Prime Minister Chang in Namgun.

The town was in an uproar over the news of the Lady of High Virtue and Chastity's arrival. Mrs. Kim went to the street and found a place to watch the parade. Soon the Lady came in a golden palanquin escorted by ten thousand soldiers in embroidered armor, with a hundred ladies-in-waiting attending in yellow-green jackets and crimson skirts adorned with seven treasures. When the company of the Lady in the golden palanquin entered the village, mysterious fragrances filled the nostrils of on-lookers and band music shook the ground.

Mrs. Kim wept at the spectacle. "Whose daughter has become such a noblewoman? If my Sukhyang had lived, would she have been such a woman?" She grew much sadder.

The Lady of High Virtue and Chastity sent a message through her lady-in-waiting to the wife of the Yangyang governor as her company entered the lodging house:

We haven't met yet. But how about having conversation to relieve our boredom under the moonlight? We need no formality as housewives.

Mrs. Kim, greatly impressed, replied:

I should have greeted you earlier. But I did not dare because such an honor is more than I deserve. Now I am very grateful for your request to meet me.

When Mrs. Kim went to the lodging house, the Lady, wearing a ceremonial coronet and decorated with seven treasures, rose from a purplish chair, made a bow, and asked her to sit on a chair to the east[105].

But Mrs. Kim refused to sit in that chair. "How could a wife of a lower post government official meet face to face with the inspector-general's wife? Please be seated comfortably."

"It's not proper for the hostess to discuss rank just to keep up her dignity. Besides, you're older than me, aren't you?"

Mrs. Kim could not resist the offer and took the chair in the east. "May I ask how old you are?" she said to the Lady.

"Twenty."

Mrs. Kim sighed.

"Why are you so sad," the Lady asked.

"I lost my daughter at the age of five during a riot and still don't know whether she is dead or alive.

---

[105] Half a line of the original text is missing—the phrase "asked her to sit" is borrowed from the Ewha Womans University Collection.

Because you're the same age as my daughter, I thought of her and grew sad."

"I lost my parents in infancy. I wonder whether my parents grieve like you when they think of me!" The Lady wept, too.

"May I dare to ask when, where, and on what occasion you parted with your parents? And who raised you to become a noblewoman?"

"I lost my parents at the age of five and wandered everywhere. Then a deer carried me on its back to the house of Prime Minister Chang. He and Lady Chang were childless, and so they raised me as a foster child."

Mrs. Kim was happy to hear about her being raised in Prime Minister Chang's house, as the Dragon King had said. But since she hadn't heard about her ordeals, she couldn't call the Lady her daughter. Instead she offered her tea. When the Lady stood up to take the cup, Mrs. Kim glimpsed a jade ring on her finger—the ring she had put on her daughter's finger.

"May I ask why you wear only one ring on your finger?" she asked.

"Before my parents left me between the rocks on Mount Panya, they tied the ring to a coat string of my dress. It isn't a pair. I've always worn it, in case I meet them."

Mrs. Kim realized the Lady was Sukhyang. She ordered her lady-in-waiting to bring her a box of cosmetics, and began to sob.

"When my husband was young, he prepared wine and food for a visit to a friend and arrived at the Pan

River. There he saw some fishermen were about to bake a turtle they had just caught. Feeling sorry for the turtle, he gave them wine and food in return for the animal and released it in the river. Much later, when he was crossing the Paegun Bridge, the bridge collapsed and he fell into the water. The turtle came to his rescue and gave him a pair of jade beads. Two letters were inscribed in each bead: one was *su* (壽), the other *pu* (福). When he married me, he sent the beads to my family as a wedding gift. My parents regarded them as precious and asked a craftsman to make a pair of rings. When I gave birth to a daughter in old age, the moon sank before me and fragrances filled the air. My husband named her Sukhyang and gave her the pen name Wŏlgung Sŏn. When she was five, bandits rioted. We escaped to Mount Panya, with the bandits chasing us. We hid our daughter between the rocks. My husband wrote down her name and the hour, date, month, and year of her birth on a piece of soft silk, placed it in a small bag with one of my jade rings, and tied it to a coat string of her dress. We haven't known her whereabouts ever since. But recently, when my husband was on his way home from a visit to the inspector-general of Hyŏngju, he met an old man, who told him the personal history of my daughter, which he wrote down. Now you're wearing the same ring I gave to my daughter Sukhyang. How could I not be sad?"

Mrs. Kim took another jade ring from the box and gave it to the Lady, with the message from the Dragon King at the Pan River. The Lady examined the ring and then came down from the chair, wailing to the sky.

"Mother, mother, I am Sukhyang!" Sukhyang took out a piece of soft silk fabric containing her name and the hour, date, month, and year of her birth and gave it to Mrs. Kim. Confirming her husband's handwriting, Mrs. Kim hugged Sukhyang, and they wept together. Three thousand ladies-in-waiting, tens of thousands of soldiers, and people from near and far, deeming the spectacle mysterious, celebrated the meeting of mother and daughter.

Kim Chŏn was checking equipment for the Lady's parade outside the residence, cautiously awaiting an order. Unexpectedly, he heard the Lady was his daughter and flew into the room, as if crazy or drunk, unable to calm his heart. He embraced Sukhyang, wailing.

"When you were imprisoned in Nagyang, I didn't recognize you because I was foolish. Now I meet you as a noblewoman. Heaven must have recognized your deep sense of filial piety." Kim could not resist his delight.

That same day, Sukhyang reported her reunion with her parents to her husband. Delighted, the inspector-general visited Yangyang in formal attire. He showed respect to his in-laws and hosted a reunion banquet lasting five days, inviting the wives of officials in Hyŏngch'o and the neighbors. Everyone who heard the news congratulated them on their reunion.

A royal advisor named Yanghoe, from Yangnŭng

District[106], heard the news during his home leave. He reported it to the Emperor upon returning to the capital. The Emperor called Duke Yi and asked him for a full account.

After hearing the story, the Emperor praised Yi Sŏn. "Since he was appointed inspector-general of Hyŏngju, bandits have become good citizens. He must have a talent for governing the whole country. He deserves a better post than an official in a province like Hyŏngju."

The Emperor issued a special order for Sŏn to be appointed Minister of Rites and Kim Chŏn inspector-general of Hyŏngju.

Upon receiving the order, Yi met with Kim Chŏn.

"The Emperor has called me to the capital," said Yi. "I'll call you to the capital as soon as possible. I wish you good luck until then."

Kim Chŏn and Mrs. Kim were sorry to part with Sukhyang, who had to follow Sŏn after parting with her parents.

"We owe all glory to you and your husband. I hope you'll invite us to the capital after you settle there." Kim grew sad.

Sukhyang also wept. "No matter what rank my husband has, nothing is more precious than living with and supporting my parents." In sorrows Sukhyang bade them farewell.

Yi sent a letter to the Emperor requesting an

---

[106] Yangnŭng District, or Yangling District (楊陵區) in Chinese, is a district of the city of Xianyang in Shaanxi Province.

audience with him at court:

> *Since my father and I share the same rank, please lower my official rank.*

Then the Emperor issued a new order:

> *Duke Yi of Wi will be appointed King of Wi in consideration of his great contribution to the country and Yi Sŏn will be Minister of Military Affairs and Duke of Ch'o[107].*

Duke Yi and Sŏn issued several appeals declining the posts, but the Emperor refused to listen to them. Finally, the two entered the palace and expressed their gratitude to him.

The Emperor asked them to tell him the story of how Sŏn met Sukhyang, after which he praised Sŏn. "All honor to you, Yi Sŏn. I know how strong your loyalty is. You should help me as faithfully as you can."

Yi Sŏn, the newly appointed Duke of Ch'o, prostrated himself on the ground. "Seeing the gifts of Kim Chŏn, he deserves a better post than inspector-general."

"I will grant him this favor in consideration of your contribution." The Emperor absolved Chang Song [108] of his crime, reinstated him as Prime Minister, and appointed Kim Chŏn Minister of Rites.

---

[107] Ch'o, or Chu (楚) in Chinese, is the name of a country.
[108] Chang Song here refers to Prime Minister Chang.

Sŏn expressed his gratitude and left the court.

After reading the royal order, Chang Song and Kim Chŏn went to the capital to express their gratitude, prostrating themselves to the Emperor.

"You owe all glory to Lady Kim of High Virtue and Chastity. You must help me and the Duke of Ch'o as faithfully as possible," the Emperor said.

The two extended their gratitude to the Emperor again and returned home.

The newly appointed Duke of Ch'o thanked the Emperor in a letter. He hosted a banquet for many kings and royal court officials.

The King of Wi lifted a glass of wine to toast Prime Minister Chang, Minister Kim, and their wives. Lady Chang described how Sahyang had wrongfully charged Sukhyang. Kim Chŏn and his wife explained how they had lost Sukhyang and searched for her. The Lady of High Virtue and Chastity recounted her past ordeals. All wept upon hearing the stories. Later, the Duke of Ch'o established the palace of the King of Wi, the mansion of Prime Minister Chang, the house of Minister Kim and Lady Yŏ all in one place and supported them all.

* * *

The King of Yang was the Emperor's third brother. He had a daughter, who was so beautiful, gifted, and excellent in writing that everyone praised her as a heroine endowed with elegance and virtue. Before his wife conceived her, an old man appeared in his dream.

"An apricot flower blossoming in the snow on Mount Pongnae will bloom in your house," he said. "Your family will prosper if you graft it upon a plum tree[109]."

As the old man predicted, his wife conceived a baby one month later and then begat a lovely daughter, whose face was as elegant as the sun and moon and whose voice was clear and silverly. The king thus named her Maehyang, meaning "the fragrance of an apricot flower," and the pen name Sŏljungmae, meaning "an apricot flower blossoming in the snow."

The King of Yang sought a son-in-law everywhere. One day he made a proposal of marriage to the family of the Duke of Yi, having heard his son was a wise man. The Duke accepted the proposal. But when he learned that Yi Sŏn had married another woman, the King of Yang was infuriated and sought other candidates. Maehyang cried.

"I've learned that a loyal official cannot serve two monarchs and a faithful wife won't serve two husbands. If I can't tie the knot with Sŏn, I'd rather die than marry another man."

"Duke Yi of Wi agreed to the marriage I proposed

---

[109] Yi (李; *li* in Chinese) is a common surname in both Korea and China. The character "yi (*li*)" also means "plum" or "plum tree." The old man's mention of an apricot flower blossoming in the snow in the King of Yang's dream foretells the birth of the princess, while the graft on a plum tree (李) augurs her marriage to a man named Yi—in this case, Yi Sŏn.

between you and Sŏn. Then Sŏn recklessly married another woman in secret, without his father's knowledge. Why are you so determined to marry him, ignoring the fact that you're growing old? With no son, I need a wise son-in-law to entrust with the future of my household. Don't resist my will by going your own way[110]."

"If you're afraid of dying without a son to carry on the family name, you can adopt one of your nephews and renounce me as your offspring. I'll support you as long as I live. But if you resist my will and force me to marry someone else, I won't continue living in this world."

The King of Yang was struggling to cope with this dilemma.

One day his wife said, "Maehyang's will is firm as a rock; even her parents can't change her mind. Now that Sŏn has become Duke of Ch'o, he can have two wives. It would be appropriate for you to ask the King of Wi to rearrange the wedding."

"It would be a shame for the princess to be a government minister's second wife. How can we do that to her?"

Maehyang said, "I wouldn't be ashamed of serving as a lady-in-waiting in the house of Sŏn, let alone his concubine. But if I marry someone from another family, it will be a shame not only for others but for me. How can I complain about becoming his second

---

[110] Part of the original sentences is missing. "Don't resist my will by going your own way" is borrowed from the National Library of Korea Collection.

wife?"

"If you think so," said the king, "I'll make another marriage proposal to the King of Wi."

The next day the King of Yang attended the assembly at court and said to the King of Wi, in the presence of the Emperor, "How could you let your son Yi Sŏn marry another woman after you promised him to my daughter?"

"I didn't break my promise," said the king, ashamed. "I was managing the affairs of state for the Emperor in the capital. My eldest sister, who was childless, raised Sŏn as her own. She orchestrated his wedding without my knowledge. This isn't my fault."

The Emperor said, "It's the will of heaven that Sŏn married the Lady of High Virtue and Chastity. So don't quarrel over this in front of me. The King of Yang should be able to find a son-in-law as nice as Sŏn."

"I wouldn't have argued with the King of Wi if things had gone smoothly in my family," said the King of Yang. "But my daughter stubbornly declared she wouldn't marry another man, because her marriage to Sŏn had already been arranged. That's why I'm so troubled."

"Yi Sŏn is a man of virtue," said the Emperor, "so he must remain faithful. Now that he is the Duke of Ch'o, he can have two wives. I hope the King of Wi will decide the matter here."

The King of Wi prostrated himself twice. "I hope Your Majesty will summon Sŏn here to order that to happen."

The Emperor sent an official to summon the

Duke of Ch'o.

The new Duke thought, "It's strange the Emperor called me to the assembly when I have no reason to participate in that meeting. I heard the King of Yang has renewed his marriage proposal to our family. The Emperor will likely settle the issue by tying the knot between our families. I'd rather not go." He thus refused to go to the palace claiming to be sick.

The Lady of High Virtue and Chastity said to the Duke, "Why are you refusing the Emperor's summons to the palace claiming to be sick. What's your reason?"

"I can't join the assembly because the Emperor will probably persuade me to accept the King of Yang's marriage proposal."

The Lady said with a serious expression, "When the Emperor summons you, you must go even it means going through fire and water. But now you refuse a royal command to take a new wife. This is not how a subject should behave."

"Of course I know it isn't right. But if the marriage proposal is accepted at court, I must have two wives, which will offend you. And if I neglect my new wife because of you, she as the princess and the Emperor-designated mate will try to use force to ruin the happiness of my family. So it's better to reject the royal proposal from the outset."

"Not true. The King of Yang made a marriage proposal, and your father accepted it when you were just a humble scholar. You secretly married me without your parents' knowledge, and I have known glory serving you and repaid my gratitude to my parents and the Prime Minister and Lady Chang. I wish for nothing more, so I won't blame you for accepting her as your proper wife and deserting me. Never fear. Even if she uses force and adopts a haughty manner, I'll treat her with benevolence and righteousness. It doesn't matter."

"I've made my decision. No need for you to be involved." He refused to go to the palace.

Hearing that the Duke was sick, the Emperor sent a court physician. The Duke lay down in bed, feigning illness. The doctor took the Duke's pulse and returned to the court, and reported to the Emperor that the Duke was sick but not serious.

The Emperor said nothing. The King of Yang was enraged.

Yi Sŏn's Journey in Search of Medicine

The empress dowager suffered from mastitis, which spread through her body, leaving her deaf, blind, and tongueless. Alarmed, the Emperor summoned the most talented physicians in the country to treat her, to no avail. The Emperor and his royal officials were very worried.

One day an ascetic visited the Emperor.

"Even such legendary physicians as Hwat'a[111] and P'yanjak[112] could not cure the empress dowager with

---

[111] Hwat'a, or Hua Tuo (華佗; c. 140–208) in Chinese, was a physician in the late Eastern Han dynasty.

[112] P'yanjak, or Bian Que (扁鵲; 407-310 BC) in Chinese,

acupuncture and medicine. She won't be able to speak until she takes the tongue-operating herb that grows on Mount Pongnae. She won't be able to hear until she takes the ear-opening grass that grows on Mount Ch'ŏnt'ae. And she won't see the world until she is treated with eye-opening beads from the Dragon King of the West Sea. Please order a virtuous court official to go and acquire these medicines."

The Emperor called all the officials at court to discuss who should go for the medicines.

The King of Yang said, "No one is as talented as Yi Sŏn. I recommend you to send him."

Both civil and military officials agreed. The Emperor called Sŏn.

"I know how faithful you are. The empress dowager is getting sicker, and no medicine on earth works. If you can acquire the legendary tongue-operating herb from Mount Pongnae, ear-opening grass from Mount Ch'ŏnt'ae, and eye-opening beads from the Dragon King of the West Sea, I'll give you half of my land."

Yi Sŏn prostrated himself twice to the Emperor. "Because I decided to devote my life to the nation as a loyal servant, if need be I will risk my life to get the medicines, though I understand that Mount Pongnae and Mount Ch'ŏnt'ae are in the southeastern and southwestern areas of heaven, respectively, while the palace of the Dragon King in the West Sea is deep underwater. It will take me at least a year to visit all

---

was a physician in the Warring States period.

three places."

Sŏn bade farewell to the Emperor, then returned home to say good-bye to his parents, Lady Yŏ, and the families of Kim Chŏn and Prime Minister Chang, who grieved as if in mourning.

Sŏn also bade farewell to the Lady of High Virtue and Chastity. "I'm dedicated to working for the state, so I must undertake this mission at the risk of my life. Don't grieve because of me. Take care of our parents in both families, as you have done for me."

"Why are you grieving, courageous man, for obeying a royal order and risking your life for the nation?" Sukhyang asked. "I'll take care of our parents with sincerity. Don't worry about them. Perform your duty in peace before you return home safe."

"But I can't promise to come home safe. If the camellia outside the window withers, it will be a sign that I'm sick. If its leaves turn yellow, then I will have met death. If all the branches turn north, then I'll come back safe."

"I'll give this as a token of my own," she said, removing a jade ring from her finger. "If the pearl in the ring turns yellow, it's a sign that I'm sick. If it turns black, then I have died."

She handed him a letter. "The old woman at the Yihwa Public House was Magu the Fairy, who gathered medicinal herbs on Mount Ch'ŏnt'ae. When you meet her, please give this to her."

Sukhyang seemed delighted, but was weeping inside. She couldn't handle her grief.

Sŏn arrived at the coast of the South Sea. The

wind blew so hard the waves reached the sky. He prepared the ritual equipment and performed a rite for the god of the sea before embarking on a vessel. Within two weeks a strong gust blew in, nearly capsizing the boat. The people on board sobbed at the prospect of their imminent deaths.

Then an enormous beast soared out of the water—a hideous creature, whose head resembled a huge gourd the size of three or four bags of rice, with four eyes and a glaring body big as a ridgepole more than one hundred *ch'ŏk*[113] tall. It roared.

"Who is so impertinent as to pass through our land without paying the toll? Give me all your treasure, or I'll devour you all."

The roaring was loud enough to turn heaven and earth upside down. Sŏn was not intimidated. Instead he prayed.

"I am Yi Sŏn, great general, governor-general, and minister of military affairs in China," he said. "The empress dowager is seriously ill, and I'm going to Mount Pongnae to acquire medicine. Please open the way."

"Maybe the minister of military affairs is cherished in your own country. But a sea monster like me couldn't care less. Stop talking nonsense. Give me your treasures."

The sea monster nearly turned the boat over. Sŏn was embarrassed.

"We have nothing but food."

He gave the beast his wife's jade ring, which

---

[113] 1 *ch'ŏk* equals approximately 30.3 centimeters.

infuriated the monster.

"This must be the eye-opening bead of the Dragon King in the West Sea. Did you steal it?"

The sea monster dragged the boat onward. The people on the boat didn't know what to do. When they arrived at a palace, the sea monster moored the vessel, grabbed everyone, and then carried them to the gate, where he reported the situation to the gatekeeper.

"I caught the man who stole the eye-opening bead of the Dragon King."

The sea monster showed the ring to a clerk inside the gate, who left, briefly, then returned.

"You must have stolen the treasure at the Dragon King's palace? What's your destination?"

"I am Yi Sŏn, minister of military affairs in China. By order of the Emperor, I am on my way to Mount Pongnae to acquire precious medicine. My wife gave me the ring when we parted. The beast ordered me to pay a toll, ridiculing me. I gave it to him because I had nothing else."

The clerk went into the palace and returned after a while.

"You said it belongs to your wife. Whose daughter is she? What's her name?"

"My wife is Sukhyang, daughter of Kim Chŏn in Nagyang."

The clerk entered the palace again. Then the people heard the Dragon King would soon come out. The palace shuddered. They saw the Dragon King emerge from the central gate, wearing a royal robe and crown and carrying a white jade scepter.

The king asked Sŏn to come closer. Yi Sŏn lay to the ground, grateful for the hospitality. The king raised him up, guided him to the floor of the Royal Palace, thanked him cordially.

"I am the Dragon King of the South Sea. How could I know you would cross this filthy area? A long time ago, my daughter committed a crime and went into exile in the Pan River. She was caught by fishermen and almost killed, but then was rescued with Kim Chŏn's help. Grateful, she gave him a pair of special jade rings. If you have a ring inscribed with the letter *bok* (福), mischievous ghosts won't hurt you. You can even escape the bad luck of being killed.

When you put a ring inscribed with the letter *su* (壽) on a dead body, its flesh won't rot for more than a thousand years. Our garrison guards are quite aware that the two pearls are the most cherished jewels in the Dragon Palace. Today one guard was patrolling the compound and sensed from far away the treasure's energy shining in the sky. So I ordered him to bring the jewel to me. Never did I expect you would be the ring bearer."

"I'm on my way to Mount Pongnae to acquire medicine for the empress dowager, who is very sick. The Emperor ordered me to get the legendary tongue-operating herb from Mount Pongnae, ear-opening grass from Mount Ch'ŏnt'ae, and an eye-opening bead from the Dragon King of the West Sea. I was crossing the water to Mt Pongnae, which is said to be in the southeastern sea. I'm very grateful to you for kindly treating such a humble person as me."

"You may not recognize me, but I know your mission quite well. When you reach Mount Pongnae, the ascetics will greet you and offer you medicine. But how can you travel as far as three thousand three hundred *li* from here?"

"What shall I do?"

"The sea routes are perilous, and you have to cross twelve countries. Be very careful."

"How far has our company come here?"

"It is some three thousand three hundred *li* from the Chinese border."

"I've already experienced indescribable hardships. How can I travel another three thousand three hundred *li*? I'm afraid I won't reach my destination."

"So far the roads have not been dangerous. But you must pass through many nations, many perilous regions, and a series of legendary rivers of hermits, including Yaksu[114]. Even a bird's feather sinks to the bottom of Yaksu. You can't cross the river by boat. If I accompany you, you can easily acquire the medicine, but I can't enter without heaven's permission. And you committed a crime in heaven that will be absolved only when you suffer ordeals on your own. You must complete this mission by yourself. But I'm worried: the roads before you are perilous."

The Dragon King threw a party for Sŏn's company. A hermit officer in the parade prostrated himself to

---

[114] Yaksu, or Ruo Shui (弱水; literally, "weak river") in Chinese, is a legendary river in old China, which had so little buoyancy that even a wild goose feather sank in it.

the king. On closer inspection, he was a youth about fifteen years old.

"Where have you been?" the Dragon King asked.

"My master said, 'You've finished learning. Now you should meet Hermit T'aeŭlsŏng. He orchestrated the operation of stars and hermit officers in heaven but committed a crime against the Great Jade Emperor. So he was exiled to the secular world and is destined to come back after living there for fifty more years. Your name will be added to the list of the hermit officers only after he returns. He will soon pass by your palace, on his way to Mount Pongnae to get medicines for the empress dowager. If you serve Hermit T'aeŭlsŏng and help him find the medicines, you'll become a hermit sooner.' So I'm here to serve Hermit T'aeŭlsŏng."

The Dragon King was very pleased.

"You see that Duke Yi is Hermit T'aeŭl you must serve. I'm relieved to hear you will support him on the way." The king told Sŏn, "The roads are very dangerous, and you'll find it hard to pass in mundane dresses. Please put on hermit robes and take my royal letters."

"Who's the boy?"

"He's my third son. He was under the tutelage of Master Ilgwang to become a hermit. Now he has come to serve you by order of his master."

"If I go with the boy," Sŏn said, delighted, "what will become of my servants?"

"I'll order the sea monster to take them by boat to the place where they were captured. They can wait there for you."

* * *

Yi Sŏn expressed his gratitude to the Dragon King, then put on the robe of a hermit officer and went to the waterside, where the prince of the Dragon King was waiting for him by a red gourd-shaped vessel. The vessel moved swiftly as an arrow, though no one was rowing.

The prince said, "I can go anywhere without being bothered by anything. But a man like you who has gone to the mundane world cannot enter the world of hermits, which is guarded by the spirits. I'll show them the royal letters from my father, the king, on which they will affix seals. You must follow my suggestions wherever you go."

"How about reaching our destination by water? The Dragon King is the supreme being in the underwater palace, isn't it? Why bother passing through so many nations on land?"

"No doubt it would be easier to go by water! If heaven knew, the dragon palace would suffer disaster and the guardian spirits in each district would also meet with calamity. I know it's burdensome, but we must pass through the nations showing our official letters."

Sŏn and the prince arrived in the country of Honŭi [115], where the people, governed by King

---

[115] An unspecified country, which, according to the Ewha Womans University Collection, is Hoehoe (回回), believed to be the empire of the Saracens—the Muslim country

Kyŏngsŏng[116], walked crabwise. The prince moored the vessel by the water's edge and entered the palace alone. The king, reading the letter, said, "Are you travelling with Hermit T'aeŭlsŏng?"

"Yes, I am."

The king affixed his signature and seal on the letter, gave it to the prince, then sent him to the waterside to greet Sŏn. The two exchanged proprieties.

They bade farewell to the king and went to the country of Hamnyŏl. The people, whose king was P'ilsŏng[117], ate only honey[118]. The king read the Dragon King's letter.

"When you serve Hermit T'aeŭlsŏng, you must be very careful: the next part of the course is the most dangerous."

The king signed the letter and returned it to Sŏn.

The two arrived in the country of Wi-wu[119]. The

---

established by Muhammad and his followers in Medina between the seventh and fifteenth centuries.

[116] Kyŏngsŏng, or Jingxing (經星) in Chinese, is a star in the second of the zodiac's twenty-eight solar stages.

[117] P'ilsŏng, or Bixing (畢星) in Chinese, is a star in the nineteenth of the zodiac's solar stages.

[118] In Sim B Collection Hamnyŏl is written as Hammil (含蜜), which is a legendary country well known for its abundance of honey.

[119] Wi-wu is written in the Ewha Womans University Collection as Yuri (琉璃), a legendary country in the eastern region of Chaozhou (潮州) and Quanzhou (泉州) in old China.

people, whose king was named Kisŏng[120], resembled the Chinese but did not eat any food that smelled fishy. When the prince showed the king the letter, the king became enraged.

"The land of hermits is different from the secular world. How could you come here?"

The king didn't pretend to look at the letter. So the prince implored him to help.

"Hermit T'aeŭlsong came down to the world and now is the minister of military affairs. By order of the Emperor, he is seeking the tongue-opening herb on Mount Pongnae and visited the Dragon King's palace. I'm escorting him. Please allow us to pass so I can save face."

"I'll allow it this time. But from now on don't ever think of acting beyond your means."

The king reluctantly signed the letter and returned it to the prince.

The two came to the country of Kyowi, where the people ate no cereal and only drank tea. They were light as birds. The prince thought it would be hard to safely pass through this land.

"The king of this country is so fastidious that not one in a thousand people can pass through the land. So you should just follow my advice."

The prince entered the palace and met the king, who asked, "What has bought the third son of the Dragon King of the South Sea here?"

---

[120] Kisŏng, or Jixing (簐星) in Chinese, is a star in the seventh of the zodiac's solar stages.

"I'm on my way to Mount Pongnae, escorting Hermit T'aeŭlsŏng to find the tongue-opening herb. I brought my father's official letter. Please let us pass through this country."

But the king was angry. "Mount Pongnae is the most celebrated mountain. Without an order from the Great Jade Emperor, even hermits don't dare enter. Hermit T'aeŭlsŏng was exalted in heaven, but he committed a crime and was exiled to the world to become a secular man. How can he enter the mountain without restrictions? Worse, your father-king and spirits allowed a secular person to enter the land of hermits without permission. I'll put you both in prison and deal with this once I receive permission from the Great Jade Emperor."

The prince implored the king to be merciful. But he wouldn't listen to him, leaving the prince disconsolate. Then the king imprisoned the prince and Sŏn in a copper castle, which looked like an underground tunnel. They couldn't even look up at the sky.

"The king of this land is so fastidious he doesn't listen to anyone," said the prince. "I'll sneak away tonight to explain this to my master. If he requests it, we may pass through."

"How can I stay in a place where I can't see even the sky? And the king will get angrier if he knows you escaped from prison? What shall we do?" Sŏn was afraid.

"No need to worry. If I go now, I'll make it back before dawn."

"Return as soon as possible." Sŏn grew even more

frightened.

The prince changed into a gust of wind, escaped from the copper castle, and visited Master Ilgwang, who was surprised to see him.

"I ordered you to escort Hermit T'aeŭl to Mount Pongnae," said the master. "What made you come back so soon?"

"Hermit T'aeŭlsŏng was caught by Kyusŏng[121] in Kyowi and is awaiting death."

Master Ilgwang laughed. "I know how fastidious he is. If I don't meet him, Hermit T'aeŭl will be put to death."

He rode on the cloud toward Kyowi, while the prince flew back to Sŏn in the copper castle.

Then Master Ilgwang rode on the Magical Super Cloud[122] and visited Kyusŏng in a flash.

"Because Hermit T'aeŭl committed a crime in heaven, the Great Jade Emperor sent him to the secular world to make him suffer. You probably know the Emperor let Hermit T'aeŭl visit Mount Pongnae to atone for his sins. Why did you imprison Hermit T'aeŭl?"

---

[121] Kyusŏng, or Kuixing (奎星) in Chinese, was the king of Kyowi or Kyoŭi (交義). Kyusŏng, Kuixing (奎星) in Chinese, is a star in the fifteenth solar stage of the zodiac.

[122] The Magical Super Cloud (筋斗雲) was what the protagonist stone monkey Sun Wukong (孫悟空) rode in Wu Cheng'en's 16th-century novel *Journey to the West*, which dramatized the legendary pilgrimage of the Tang dynasty Buddhist priest Xuanzang to India to obtain Buddhist sutras.

"I know all this. I imprisoned him in the copper castle so that he would suffer for a long time. But how did you know this?"

"I heard it from my disciple—the son of the Dragon King in the South Sea."

"I'll release them after three days so that they suffer excruciating pain."

"Time is running out: the empress dowager is very sick. If Hermit T'aeŭl accomplishes his duty belatedly, he will suffer another ordeal. I ask you to allow him to leave."

Kyusŏng called the prince and Sŏn. "Living in the secular world, you committed the grave sin of entering and ruining the land of hermits. I planned to jail you for ten thousand years, but I'll free you at Master Ilgwang's request." Kyusŏng reluctantly signed the document.

When the prince arrived at the water's edge with Sŏn, he saw five clouds forming a pillar, atop which were two hermit officers enjoying the scenery.

"Who on earth are they? And how can they enjoy art in the air?" Sŏn asked.

"The man sitting to the east is Master Ilgwang and the one in the west is Kyusŏng."

Sŏn expressed his gratitude many times in Master Ilgwang's direction.

"No need to envy them," said the prince. "We'll become hermits like them sooner or later."

They reached another country named Wu-o, where the people were more than ten *ch'ŏk* tall and ate animals or human flesh rather than boiled rice.

"During my visit to the king, the people will

attempt to devour you. You must throw this talisman." The prince entered the country to meet the king.

The king was so wise he read the Dragon King's letter and immediately signed it. "The people of this land are cruel by nature. Please take care of yourself."

Indeed they tried to devour Yi Sŏn on the boat. In fear he threw them the prince's talisman, which gave rise to a sudden gale and high waves. When they fell into the water and floundered, the boat rapidly sailed upwind. Sŏn had nothing else to do. He let the boat sail where it willed.

Truths of the Past Unveiled

At the same time a hermit was riding a whale, walking on water.

The hermit said to Sŏn, "You appear to be neither a hermit nor a man in the mundane world, much less the Dragon King. How do you get his gourd vessel? Where are you heading?"

Sŏn prostrated himself to the hermit. "I am Yi Sŏn, minister of military affairs in China. Because the empress dowager is seriously ill, I'm on my way to Mount Pongnae to acquire tongue-opening herb by order of the Emperor. I wish you would show me the way."

The hermit officer laughed. "You say you're minister of military affairs. But perhaps you didn't read the classics. The three legendary mountains of hermits and ten islands of hermits are just a fantasy. Didn't you hear that with all of their authority even the First Emperor of Qin and Emperor Mu of Han couldn't find Mount Pongnae? Don't believe empty talk. Just follow me to enjoy the beautiful scenery and search for taverns."

"Your suggestion makes sense. But as a royal subject I have to follow the Emperor's order, I can't stop halfway. If after risking my life I can't acquire the medicine, I'll accept that result. Please show me the way."

"I can go ninety-seven thousand *li* in a second riding a whale. But I've never seen or heard of Mount Pongnae. Stop this foolish quest and follow me to get a drink."

He steered the boat eastward, saying things that upset Sŏn. Another hermit officer riding a plantain flower, with a green sword on his shoulder, approached them, wavering to the wind.

"Hey, Yi Chŏksŏn, where have you been?" he said.

"This boy is harassing me to take him to a drinking house. I'm leading him to a tavern in a bamboo forest."

The new official laughed. "He's a secular man, but he must be a reliable friend to look for a tavern at his leisure. Hey, brother. Do you have any money?"

"I'm just a humble man in the secular world," said Yi Sŏn. "I've come for the tongue-opening herb on Mount Pongnae, by order of the Emperor. I've gone through hell and high water to get here. But I don't know what to do because this hermit is holding me."

"Don't you know his name? He's Yi T'aebaek[123], a National Academy scholar in the Tang dynasty. You need ten thousand jars of wine to get him drunk. Do you have enough money?"

"I left my servants with a sea monster, and came here with the son of the Dragon King in the South Sea. But I parted with him, and don't have enough money for a bottle of wine."

"Why don't you sell your wife's jade ring to buy me a drink?" Yi Chŏkson made fun of Sŏn.

They heard the sound of a jade pipe in the distance. Yi Chŏkson said, "Yŏ Tongbin, my friend, do you know who the piper is? It's Wang Chagyun[124]? Let's see where he's going."

Yi Chŏkson urged the whale forward fast as the wind, making a thunderous noise.

A hermit officer was playing a pipe on a zither floating on the water. Noticing Sŏn, he said, "Glad to see you! T'aeŭl. How are you getting along in the mundane world?"

Sŏn prostrated to the player twice. "I'm on my way to Mount Pongnae to get tongue-opening herb by order of the Emperor. It's a pleasure to see the beautiful scenery with your fellow hermit officers. But I'm perplexed because your friends won't let me

---

[123] Yi T'aebaek (李太白) is another name for Yi Chŏkson. The text again uses Yi Chŏkson hereafter.

[124] Wang Chagyun, or Wang Zijun (王子均) in Chinese, was a 6th-century BC prince, who became a hermit after thirty years of practice on Mount Song in Henan Province, China.

go. I have to hurry."
Yi Chŏkson laughed. "This traveler insists on buying me a drink, keeping hold on me even after dark. He'll sell off his wife's jade ring to pay for it. I'm in big trouble." "Hermit T'aeŭl says he was caught by Yi Chŏkson and Yi Chŏkson says the opposite. Who's telling the truth?" Yŏ Tongbin laughed, and then they all laughed together.
The sight of a fairy bearing jars of wine on a lotus leaf boat prompted Yŏ Tongbin to ask, "Where are you going?"
"I heard that Master Tu Mokchi will meet his old friend in the Galaxy," she said. "I'm on my way there."
"He'd probably like to meet Hermit T'aeŭl." Wang Chagyun said.
"Tu Mokchi won't spare wine for us anyway." Yi Chŏkson said, then ordered the fairy to give him wine, which she did, unwillingly. Yi Chŏkson filled his glass to the brim.
"If we drink this glass of wine without offering it to our friend, he'll feel bored. But if I pour wine into a bag filled with human shit and blood[125], he'll get butterflies in his stomach."
"You must know he was once a wine bag. I'm afraid his stomach will burst if we pour wine into it," Yŏ Tongbin said with a laugh.
"If it bursts, we can sew him up with horsehair stitches," said Wang. "Let's try it."

---

[125] This is a metaphor for Yi Sŏn, who had become a mundane person.

The three hermit officers made fun of Sŏn in every way. Sŏn sat still, ashamed, unable to speak. Soon another hermit officer riding a lion approached from the west.

"Why are you harassing my friend?" The newcomer caught Sŏn's hand. "The prince who escorted you is wandering about after losing track of you. I told him, 'Yi Chŏkson is with Yi Sŏn. Believe me. Report to all the kings of the twelve kingdoms and then go directly to Mount Pongnae.' No need to worry. Just come with me to the mountain after you finish your wine."

Sŏn, delighted, expressed his gratitude.

"You don't recognize us?" said the newcomer.

"How can a person in the mundane world see you clearly with his blind eyes?"

"The master over there is Wang Chagyun, this friend is Yŏ Tongbin, and next to him is Yi Chŏkson. I'm Tu Mokchi. In heaven, we were all on intimate terms. After you went to the secular world, we missed you terribly. Some days ago, Master Ilgwang said, 'Hermit T'aeŭl is tormented by the kings of the twelve kingdoms on his way to Mount Pongnae.' So I secured a leave of absence to come here from the Great Jade Emperor. Yi Chŏkson was just teasing you to check your reaction. No offense. Don't blame him too much."

Sŏn prostrated himself to him. "I'm very grateful to you for coming here to meet me. How could I blame them for teasing me?"

"Hermit T'aeŭl used to look down on us in heaven," Tu Mokchi said. "Never did we imagine he would respect his old friends with sincerity."

The officials offered wine to each other.

A hermit-attending boy in a blue robe, riding a crane, arrived at the scene. "Animi Saeng[126] invites you to the castle of Chingnyŏ[127] today," he said.

"How can we refuse a senior friend's request? But I wonder if we should bring T'aeŭl there or not," Yŏ Tongbin said.

"When I was coming here, I saw Chang Kŏn[128] going to Mount Pongnae," Tu Mokchi said. So I exchanged my crane for his lion. The mountain isn't far. I'll take Hermit T'aeŭl there and exchange Chang Kŏn's lion for my crane. You go there first. I'll follow soon."

Pleased, they said to Sŏn, "We came here to meet you because it's been a long time since you left. But now we must part with you at the invitation of our old friend. We're sorry to leave you again so soon. *Bon voyage.* We'll meet each other before long."

The three hermit officers left.

Sŏn followed Tu Mokchi to the southeast, where he saw a huge mountain surrounded by five-color clouds.

Tu Mokchi said, "That's Mount Pongnae. But I

---

[126] An'gi Saeng, or Anqi Sheng (安期生) in Chinese, was a Chinese immortal believed to have lived for over a thousand years.
[127] The legendary castle where Chingnyŏ (Zhinüm) lived.
[128] Chang Kŏn, or Zhang Qian (張騫) in Chinese, was a Chinese official and diplomat in the second century BC in the Han dynasty.

wonder whether you can climb it?"

"Do I have to go to the peak to get the medicine?"

"On the highest peak lives Hermit Kuru. You should ask him for the medicine."

They arrived at the foot of the mountain. The prince was waiting at the water's edge.

"You've come to Mount Pongnae and met the prince again. I have to leave now." Tu Mokchi said. He rode the lion into the sky.

"Where have you been?" Sŏn asked the prince.

"After securing the document and the King of Wu-o's signature, I went to the water's edge. When I found that you had already left, I searched for you here and there. Then I met Tu Mokchi, who told me he had met you and asked me to come to Mount Pongnae after reporting to the twelve kings. I've been waiting for you for a long time."

"Those hermit officers kept making fun of me. It scared the hell out of me."

"Those hermit officers were your friends in your previous life. They poked fun at you as a way of greeting you. Had you not met them, you wouldn't have met half of the twelve kings."

The prince attended Sŏn up the mountain until they came to a precipitous cliff, the top of which reached the sky. "How can we climb those rocks?" Sŏn asked.

"Don't worry," said the prince. "Just ride on my back."

Sŏn climbed on the back of the prince, who changed into a yellow dragon, soared into the sky, and ascended to the top of the mountain.

"You're extraordinary," said Sŏn.
"We've reached our destination. I'll keep the boat at the water's edge. Enter the valley to meet Hermit Kuru, and come back to the river with the tongue-opening medicine."
"How will I get down the mountain with the medicine?"
"The way back won't be difficult. Don't worry."
The prince climbed down from the peak.

* * *

Yi Sŏn went into the valley alone. A greying old man riding a black cow approached him.
"Who are you?"
"I'm Yi Sŏn, minister of military affairs in China, here to meet Hermit Kuru." Sŏn prostrated himself twice.
"Enter the base of that agarwood tree. You'll find hermit officers playing go[129] on a lofty rock. Ask them."
Sŏn went there and saw jade rocks surrounded by five-colored clouds. Everything was in bloom, and Nan[130] and Ponghwang[131], peacocks, blue and white

---

[129] *Go* (圍棋; literally "encircling game"; *paduk* in Korean), a board game involving two players, which originated in China more than 2,500 years ago.

[130] Nan, or Luan (鸞) in Chinese, is a fabulous bird that is said to resemble a phoenix.

[131] Ponghwang, or Fenghuang (鳳凰) in Chinese, is the

cranes, all rambled about in pairs. This was what they called the world of hermits.

"Who said the three legendary mountains are fabrication? I can see one with my own eyes." Yi Sŏn, admiring the view, walked on to see two hermit officers, one in a red and the other in a blue robe, playing *go* on a lofty rock. Sŏn prostrated himself from a distance, but the two were indifferent to him. He came nearer, but they still pretended not to see him. Sŏn didn't know what to do. Then a boy in a blue dress brought tea and reported his presence to the hermit officers. "You have a guest from a secular world over there."

Surprised, they looked around and pushed the *go* board aside.

"Who are you? Why have you come to screw up the scenery of the hermit world?" one asked.

"I'm Yi Sŏn, minister of military affairs in China. I came here to meet Hermit Kuru." Sŏn prostrated himself twice.

"Why are you looking for him?" The hermit officer in the blue robe asked.

"I have come here to acquire tongue-opening herb by order of the Emperor."

"You can meet him only after climbing the peak. But can you in a human body do that?" asked the hermit officer in a red robe.

Yi saw that the rock to find was three thousand *kil* high and steep as ice sculpture. He felt embarrassed,

---

mythological phoenix of East Asia. Males and females were called *feng* and, *huang*, respectively.

because it seemed impossible for him to scale that even if he had wings.

"I pray you help me," Sŏn said.

"You asked me to tell you where Hermit Kuru is, and I did. But now you can't climb the rock. What shall we do?" said the hermit officer in the blue robe.

"It was good luck that you came up here from the mundane world. How do you expect to go to a more dangerous place? How about playing *go* with us instead of seeking Hermit Kuru?" said the hermit officer in the red robe.

Sŏn prostrated himself twice. "It was good luck for me to bring my corrupted body here. But the Emperor's orders mean I must fulfil my mission. Please help me find the medicine."

"We're hermits just enjoying the scenery. We don't know about this medicine." The hermit officer in the blue robe poked fun at Sŏn.

A new hermit officer riding a yellow crane arrived and said, "You should have greeted this old friend of yours. Why are you making so much fun of him?"

The newcomer, Hermit Kuru, clutched Sŏn's hand. "It's nice to meet you, Hermit T'aeŭl. How are you getting along in the secular world? Sŏljungmae[132] went down to the world to see you. Have you met her?"

"I, Yi Sŏn, suffered much in the world. I had no fun, nor did I ever hear of Sŏljungmae."

"Hermit T'aeŭl must have forgotten what

---

[132] Sŏljungmae here refers to Maehyang, the daughter of the King of Yang.

happened in heaven." Hermit Kuru laughed. He ordered an attendant-boy to bring tea to Sŏn.

Sŏn drank, remembering his past: how he committed a crime in heaven and went into exile in the world; how he secured a leave of absence from the Great Jade Emperor, enjoyed his time on Mount Pongnae, and married Sŏljungmae, daughter of Hermit Nŭnghŏ; he had been a friend of the two hermit officers to his left and right. Sŏn sobbed.

"My sin was so heavy I have suffered many ordeals in the mundane world!"

"Sŏljungmae, the daughter of Nŭnghŏ the ascetic, was born again as the daughter of the King of Yang. She is destined to be your second wife."

"I wondered what made Sŏljungmae come down to the world! Why was Soa born to Kim Chŏn when Sŏljungmae was the daughter of the King of Yang?"

"Long ago, Master Nŭnghŏ and his wife went to Mount Pangjang to sightsee. He offered the wrong tangerines to heaven, so he was exiled to the world. Master Nŭnghŏ was born to Master Unsu in Namyang. His wife was born to Chang Ho in Yŏngch'ŏn. Master Nŭnghŏ felt bitter toward Soa because T'aeŭl, enamored of Soa, didn't care about Sŏljungmae. Soa was thus born to Master Nŭnghŏ and worried him for fifteen years from the age of five. Sŏljungmae drowned herself in the river of Yaksu so as to meet you in the world. Thus she was born as the daughter of the King of Yang and raised in a noble family."

"If that's the case, Sŏljungmae must have been my wife. But why did I meet Soa first?"

"You went down to the world because of Soa, who was a fairy favored by Wŏlgung Hang'a. Hang'a reluctantly sent Soa into the world, so you had to take care of her. Soa thus became your first wife. When both of you turn seventy, you will return to heaven together."

"I came a long way because I declined the King of Yang's marriage proposal. Though I was determined to reject the proposal, I now know I can't avoid a heaven-designated tie." Sŏn remembered what happened in heaven and forgot all about the secular world.

"It's time for you to go home. Please take this medicine with you."

"What's the name of this medicine?"

"I put the nectar of reincarnation in the iron bowl. The plant is the tongue-opening herb. And this pill will cause a dead person to be reborn as a hermit. If you put your jade ring on the dead body, rotten flesh will change into fresh skin. If the dead drink the nectar, they will regain soul and spirit. If the sick eat the tongue-opening herb, they will regain their speech."

"What are these pills for?"

"Treasure them carefully until you turn seventy. Then eat one each with Soa at noon on the fifteenth day of July that year." The hermit offered Sŏn another cup of tea.

Yi drank it, remembering that the prince was waiting for him by the river. He had to hurry up the process of returning to the secular world. He bade farewell to the hermit officers before leaving. The hermits escorted him to the river to send him off.

"We wish we had spent more time together. Please visit us when you return to heaven."

Sŏn was greeted by the prince.

"The way back is different from our journey here. Please close your eyes for a moment after riding on the boat."

Sŏn blinked, and the vessel reached the Dragon Palace of the South Sea in an instant.

* * *

The Dragon King greeted Yi Sŏn by throwing a party for him.

"With your help, I made it back from Mount Pongnae," Sŏn said. "Now please show me the way to Mount Ch'ŏnt'ae."

"You can visit Mount Ch'ŏnt'ae easily, because it isn't far from the mundane world. But you will find it hard to meet Magu the Fairy."

The king called the prince. "You must escort Sŏn to Mount Ch'ŏnt'ae. You should also visit the P'yojin River in the Western Sea, acquire the eye-opening bead from my sister, and give it to Sŏn. Then you should visit your master before you come back."

Obeying the order, the prince escorted Sŏn to a certain place. "We're on Mount Ch'ŏnt'ae," he said. "Go around this mountain to find Magu the Fairy, who will give you the medicine. I'll go to the P'yojin River in the Western Sea to get the eye-opening bead."

Sŏn agreed, watching Mount Ch'ŏnt'ae, where tens of millions of multi-layered mountains rose high in the air.

"If I meet a ferocious beast in such rugged mountains, how will I avoid death?" Sŏn said.

"Don't worry," said the prince. "This is a celebrated mountain where no such animals live. But you should respect anyone you meet with sincerity. Don't think of anything vexatious. If you make a mistake, you'll find it hard to come back here."

Sukhyang and Yi Sŏn Return to Heaven

After parting from the prince, Sŏn went into the mountains. When he came to a river, there was no bridge over the deep water, and as he wandered about, searching for a way across, a boy riding a deer approached from the east. When Sŏn approached, the boy kicked the deer, which ran at full speed until it vanished. Sŏn followed the deer into the mountains, finding no trace of humans, roaming here and there, until he found a beggar-like old man in quilted clothes, seated on a rock under a big pine tree. He prostrated himself to the old man.

"Could you tell me where Magu the Fairy is?"

"I've been here for more than fifty-eight thousand years, and I never heard that name."

"Are there any houses nearby? I'm dying of hunger. I have to eat something."

"Who would expect to find a house deep in the mountains?"

The old man stood up and went away. Sŏn tried to follow him, but he was already gone. He was sitting by the river, unable to cross, when a Buddhist monk walked past, carrying a six-ring staff [133]. Sŏn prostrated himself with courtesy.

"I'm looking for Magu the Fairy. Where can I meet her?"

"Why are you looking for her?"

"I'm Yi Sŏn, minister of military affairs in China. I've come to acquire ear-opening grass by order of the Emperor. I heard I have to meet Magu the Fairy to get it."

"Cross this river and go east. You can find Okp'o-dong. Seek her there."

"But I can't cross the river. The water is deep and there is no bridge. Please help me."

The monk threw his stick into the river, with six ritual rings attached, and it changed into a bridge, which Sŏn crossed, then expressed his gratitude. The monk rode up on a cloud, saying, "I'm the Buddha of the Taesŏng Temple. I've come to show you the way to Okp'o-dong."

"How can I meet her?" Sŏn said, prostrating himself.

"You'll meet her soon. In any event, the empress dowager has died. You must hurry to get the medicine and go back to the palace."

Sŏn expressed his gratitude to the Buddhist monk and headed east. He found on the way all sorts of mysterious flowers and trees, as well as spring flowers and laurel trees standing in line. The cries of

---

[133] The staff of a Buddhist monk, the top of which is made of metal; metal rings are fixed to it so as to rattle. It is called *yukhwanjang* or *sŏkjang* in Korean.

strange beasts flocking together saddened him. He couldn't see the way clearly, because thick five-colored clouds shrouded the mountains, which were folded in layers. He went deeper yet, and still he couldn't find any house, which bewildered him.

Sŏn saw an old man perching on a rock, approached to him and prostrated himself twice.

"I'm heading for Okp'o-dong. Could you tell me where it is?"

The old man sang a song:

One thousand years is a moment for me and ten thousand years is a day.
I travel the four seas and eight directions in a flash.
But who on earth dares to ask me the way?

The old man closed his eyes and lay on a rock. He didn't breathe, as if dead. Sŏn couldn't ask him anything more, so he continued walking to the east.

Now he saw a woman riding in a jade wagon led by a white deer. She had a heavenly peach in her hand. Her hair was white as snow, and her face was gorgeous as a peach blossom.

Sŏn lay flat on the ground and, without looking up, said, "May I ask you to tell me the way to Okp'o-domg?"

The old woman hurried down from the cart. "Who are you?" she said. "Why are you going to Okp'o-domg?"

Sŏn prostrated himself twice.

"I'm Yi Sŏn, minister of military affairs in China. Because the empress dowager is seriously ill, I've come to acquire ear-opening grass from Mountain Ch'ŏnt'ae by order of the Emperor. I heard that Magu the Fairy has the medicine."

"You must have taken a wrong turn. I've lived on this mountain for four hundred and eighty-nine thousand and four hundred and fifty-seven years, I know every place here. But I have never heard of Magu the Fairy and Okp'o-domg, let alone the mountain."

"What's the name of this mountain? Please tell me?" Sŏn said, alarmed.

"This is Mount P'o-ok[134]. This valley is called T'aech'ŏn-dong[135]. You're on the wrong path, and it's already dark. It will be hard to go back, and there's no private house nearby. Why don't you stay in my house tonight and look for Mount Ch'ŏnt'ae tomorrow?"

"Where is Mount Ch'ŏnt'ae?"

"I have no idea."

She took him to a valley filled with five-colored rock and a thousand different kinds of flowers, infused with a strange energy. The ground was embroidered with thin, flat five-colored stones. Sŏn was afraid to step on them. Going deeper into the

---

[134] The original name in Chinese, P'o-ok (瀑玉), is made in a reversed arrangement of Okp'o (玉瀑), Okp'o and the place unit of dong being changed into a mountain. It is also interpreted as a trick or linguistic pun.

[135] T'aech'ŏn is a reversed form of Ch'ŏnt'ae. Here the original name of the mountain has been changed into the name of a valley.

valley, he saw a house and smelled a mysterious fragrance there. On closer inspection, the house was majestic as a palace. The old woman got off the cart and led him inside.

"Because I'm a widow living in this house, I have no one to serve an honorable guest like you, and so I'll serve you. Please don't blame me. Just step onto the hall."

Sŏn declined her offer. "I'm only a filthy man from the secular world, who's worried about contaminating this precious house. How can I go onto the hall and sit before you? I'd rather take shelter under the eaves and leave here tomorrow after daybreak."

The old woman smiled. "I know a grown-up man and woman are not allowed to sit together face to face. But I'm so old it doesn't matter. This house isn't dirty, and you have nowhere to go. Don't decline my offer. Come onto the hall."

Sŏn went onto the hall. The old woman took out two golden chairs, one for the east and one for the west. She asked him to sit in the east chair. This he refused to do so.

"If you accept my proposal, you'll get the medicine. If not, you won't return home alive."

"What do you mean? I'll listen to you if it's worth it. But I won't follow your suggestion, if it puts my life at risk."

"I was the wife of a celebrity[136], living in splendor.

---

[136] The Ewha Womans University Collection notes the old woman's husband was a celebrity in the Tang dynasty.

But my husband committed a crime against the nation and was exiled here. After he passed away, I supported myself by farming. Regrettably, my daughter, who is past marriageable age, remains single. But now that I have finally met you, I think you must be her heaven-sent partner. She isn't that pretty, but is more than qualified to be your wife. Please don't reject my offer."

"But the empress dowager's illness is extremely serious. The Emperor wishes me to return with the medicine as soon as possible. If I indulge myself in wine and pleasure without regard for his order, heaven will punish me. How can I expect to live after committing a crime against heaven? I'd rather die now without regret. I'm sorry I won't take your suggestion."

"If you can get the medicine and revive the empress dowager, you'll be promoted to a higher government position and enjoy great wealth. If you go back emptyhanded, you won't avoid the disaster that befell General So Ong[137]. Conventional wisdom says a diseased prime minister is no better than a living pig. Even First Emperor of Qin and Emperor Mu of Han failed to find the elixir of life, despite their power. Where on earth can you get the medicine, even if you devote your heart and soul to the quest? I'm not rich, but I have 108,000 *majigi* of rice paddies and fields; 42,700 servants; and 87,900

---

[137] So Ong, or Shao Weng (少翁) in Chinese, was a master of occult arts in the Qi dynasty.

mulberry trees; also 107,000 pots of silver in the treasure house to the east; 45,000 pots of gold in the repository in the west; 900,000 pieces of silk in the southern warehouse; and countless carts containing pearls and other jewels in the northern storehouse. So you can remain jobless until your death and still not worry. Please accept my proposal."

The old woman called her daughter and sat her down beside Yi Sŏn, who was seized with fear. Not knowing what to do, he lowered his blue hood to glance at her. He wasn't certain, but she looked like his wife, the Lady of High Virtue and Chastity, which pleased him until he remembered the prince's advice. Then he adamantly refused to greet her.

The girl entered the room, saying, "The empress dowager has passed away. Government officials have lodged an appeal with the Emperor, arguing our family must be punished. The Emperor is still waiting for you, though. You'd better hurry back with the medicine."

Sŏn realized his wife had come to see him. He was about to talk to her, but she had gone inside. He returned to the guest room and went to sleep.

When he woke, the house was gone, and he saw only a pavilion under a pine tree by the stream. Curious, Yi Sŏn left, reciting a poem. A ragged old woman was digging up edible plants with a *sapsari* beside her. Sŏn approached and bowed to her.

"Where is Mount Ch'ŏnt'ae located?" he said.

"We are on that very mountain," she replied.

"Where is Okp'o-dong?"

"You've just come from that place."

"Where is Magu the Fairy?" Sŏn was excited. She put her hand on her brow, looking at Sŏn.

"I'm sorry but my eyes are too weak for me to recognize you. Who on earth are you? I'm Grandma Magu the Fairy."

Delighted, Sŏn prostrated himself twice to the old woman. "Don't you recognize me? I'm Yi Sŏn, the son of Duke Yi of Wi in Northern Village in Nagyang. I've come to get medicine by order of the Emperor."

Yi gave her a letter sent by his wife.

Grandma Magu showed her real face. "How is Sukhyang? Considering the relationship between Sukhyang and me, I have neither reservations nor regrets about giving this medicinal herb of eternal youth to you. Had you renounced your faith in showing sincerity, your efforts might have been fruitless. But thanks to your devotion, perhaps, the herb has sprouted."

She gave him a mushroom. "I heard from Kim Sukhyang that the empress dowager had already died. You must hurry back to the palace." And then she vanished.

Yi prostrated himself a number of times in the direction of Okp'o-dong and then returned to the river, where the prince was waiting for him.

"I met my aunt in the P'yojin River in the Western Sea and asked her for an eye-opening bead. She said, 'I had two eye-opening beads. But I gave one to Kim Chŏn in Nagyang to repay my gratitude to him, and the other to the Lady of High Virtue and Chastity when she came to perform rituals in the P'yojin River.

Thus the two beads are already in the possession of Kim's family.' I've come back emptyhanded," the prince said. "Please close your eyes."

Yi Sŏn, seated on the dragon-design vessel, closed his eyes. Soon they came to a river called Kyehwe[138] outside the royal palace gate. Sŏn went ashore and parted from the prince.

"We went through many hardships in the wide, wide sea before returning to our country. It's sad to part." Sŏn shared the prince's sorrow. "Farewell until we meet again."

Yi Sŏn, arriving at the royal palace, heard the empress dowager had been dead for twenty days. Her body was considerably disfigured. Feeling bitter, Yi entered the palace, carrying a jade ring. The simultaneous cries of government officials shuddered heaven and earth.

Yi Sŏn approached the empress dowager with different kinds of medicine. When he put the jade ring on her finger, her flesh soon recovered its color. After putting the ear-opening herb in her ears, Yi Sŏn cleaned her eyes with the eye-opening bead. Her eyes and body regained their splendor. Soon she sat up in bed, as if awakened from sleep.

The Emperor was amazed and pleased. He took Sŏn by the hand, weeping. "I was so worried when I

---

[138] The River Kyŏnghwa in the Ewha Womans University Collection.

sent you to the wide, wide land and sea. Now that you have come back to miraculously save the empress dowager's life, my happiness is beyond compare. You got the medicine that even the First Emperor of Qin and Emperor Mu of Han failed to get. How can I forget my promise to you?"

The Emperor said he would give Yi Sŏn half of the country.

But Yi lay down on the ground, sobbing. "I paid my due respect to Your Majesty, obeying your order because you attended the empress dowager with such devotion. If you divide the country in two and give me half, I will gain a bad reputation in the future. If you still insist, I'd rather die in your presence before I see my parents, my wife, and children."

Yi reverently bent his head down to the ground. He asked the Emperor to punish him for the crime of disobeying the royal decree.

Moved by his loyalty, the Emperor appointed him King of Ch'o.[139] Yi Sŏn expressed his gratitude to the Emperor, and returned home.

He prostrated himself twice to his parents, who, like his relatives and neighbors, junior and senior, young and old alike, greeted him as if they had seen a dead man coming back to life.

Smiling, Sukhyang said with a clear ringing voice, "After you left us, the camellia outside the window

---

[139] The original text says the Emperor appointed the Duke of Wi as King of Wi at the same time. The translation has not rendered the sentence because the nomination had already been made. This must be a textual error.

grew briskly, all its branches turning north. I thus knew you would come back safely. One day Grandma Magu took me somewhere in a dream, where I met you and sent you the news. You've come back so quickly, and I am really happy."

Meantime the Emperor awarded many prizes to the King of Ch'o and sent court musicians for a special banquet to celebrate this reunion.

The King of Yang wanted Yi Sŏn to hasten the marriage to his daughter. The newly appointed King of Ch'o couldn't resist the offer because of what he had heard from a hermit officer on Mount Pongnae. He went to the royal family of the King of Yang, held a wedding, and returned after three days, escorted by the armed soldiers of Yang. Everyone envied him, including royal officials, for the King of Ch'o was now richer than anybody else.

The Emperor appointed Maehyang Queen of Fidelity, and she gave birth to three sons and two daughters. Sukhyang, now the Queen of High Virtue and Chastity[140], had two sons and a daughter, all of them outstanding in terms of countenance and skill. Her daughter became the wife of the Crown Prince, while the eldest son became Prime Minister. The second son became the governor of Sŏryang and minister of defense. He defeated all the barbarians

---

[140] A text in the Ewha Womans University Collection notes that the Emperor appointed Sukhyang, the Lady of High Virtue and Chastity, as the Queen of High Virtue and Chastity, which makes sense, since Yi Sŏn had become the King of Ch'o.

in the north and south, successfully ruled over the bandits, and was amply rewarded by the Emperor.

* * *

Time passed. Prime Minister and Lady Chang and Lady Yŏ passed away. The King of Ch'o held a funeral service with propriety. Alas! Before long, his parents died. The King of Ch'o buried them in the family tomb with proper rituals and mourned the dead for three years.

The mourning period passed. One day the King of Ch'o brought his five children to the court garden for an archery competition. The Queen of High Virtue and Chastity watched, drawing bead curtains. She saw an old soldier, who looked like the bandit who had saved her on Mount Panya and taken her to a valley. When she told the king, he summoned the soldier.

"Did you save someone on Mount Panya a long time ago?"

The old soldier thought for a while. "Yes, I remember finding a little girl weeping between the rocks. She had lost her parents. I thought she would become a great figure. Lest she be eaten by beasts, I brought her to the entrance of a remote mountain village."

When the king told this story to the queen, she was pleased. She called the man to tell her story and asked the king to give him lots of prizes.

Time passed. The King of Ch'o turned seventy. On the fifteenth day of July, on the lunar calendar in the Year of Musul, Yi Sŏn the King and Sukhyang the Queen of High Virtue and Chastity went up to the Wanwŏl Pavilion to see the beauty of the moon. Then five-colored clouds reared on high into the air and a hermit officer came down from heaven. Yi Sŏn hurriedly rose up to greet him, discovering that he was Yŏ Tongbin.

"Where are you coming from?"

"Have you forgotten what day it is? Today is the day you are destined to ascend to heaven. But I wonder whether you can go up to heaven with that body."

Yi Sŏn remembered the two pills that Hermit Kuru had given him. He took them out and ate them with Sukhyang. The pills made their bodies light enough to fly and forget all of their mundane affairs. They rode on a cloud following Yŏ and ascended into heaven.

Kim Chŏn and his wife were sad when Yi Sŏn and Sukhyang went to heaven. One day on a boat ride with the Queen of Fidelity, a hermit officer approached with three orange-like fruits.

"You each must eat one." When Kim took them, the hermit added, "You forgot all heavenly things when you came down to earth."

The fruit they ate lightened their bodies, and they flew directly to Mount Pongnae without saying farewell to their families.

When the Emperor heard the news, he thought this strange and praised them.

"Heaven has sent hermit officers and fairies to help me."

The Emperor summoned all government officials and ordered them to perform memorial services at the state shrines for Kim Chŏn, the King of Ch'o, and the King of Wi. This story is recorded in an unofficial book of history.

Sugyŏng's Tale

Main Characters

- **Sugyŏng:** Formerly a fairy, she was expelled from heaven for her crime. She is destined to meet Sŏn'gun, her heaven-sent mate, and waits for him. After marriage, she is wrongfully accused of infidelity by her father-in-law.
- **Paek Sŏn'gun:** Son of Minister Paek. Like Sugyŏng, he was expelled from heaven for his crime. He marries his heaven-sent woman Sugyŏng. After passing the civil service examination, he takes revenge on those who slandered his wife.
- **Minister Paek:** A former government minister, Paek welcomes Sugyŏng as his daughter-in-law. But after his son Sŏn'gun travels to the capital to take the civil service examination, he suspects Sugyŏng of infidelity. His full name is Paek Sŏkju.
- **Lady Paek:** Wife of Minister Paek. When her husband suspects their daughter-in-law of infidelity, she recognizes her innocence and persuades him to forgive her.
- **Maewŏl:** A maid servant in Minister Paek's house. She once served Sŏn'gun and loved him. After Sŏn'gun's marriage to Sugyŏng, she is tormented by his indifference and plots to slander Sugyŏng when Sŏn'gun is away.
- **Tolsoe:** A male slave in Minister Paek's house. Treacherous and covetous, he helps Maewŏl carry out her evil scheme in return for a huge sum of money.

The list of the names and the explanations in "Main Characters" are not part of the original text but have been added by translators in order to help readers understand the story better.

Encounter of Two Heaven-sent Lovers

Once upon a time, in the Koryŏ dynasty, a government official named Paek Sŏkju lived in the eastern part of Kyŏngsang-do[141]. A descendent of the scholar-cum-government minister Paek P'yŏng, he passed the civil service examination as a boy and served as vice-minister of defense. Falsely accused of wrongdoing by fellow government officials, he gave up his position and returned home to devote himself to farming and accumulating wealth. At forty, though, he was sad over the fact that he was childless.

One day Lady Paek told him, "Of the many crimes in human affairs, the failure to give birth to a child is the gravest. How will I face my ancestors when I die? I should already have been kicked out of the house. But I still live with you thanks to your generosity. I'm indebted to you. If couples pray devoutly on the summit of Mount Sobaek[142], it's said their dream will be fulfilled. Why don't we climb that peak and make our prayers to the mountain spirit[143]?"

---

[141] Kyŏngsang-do (慶尙道), in the Korean peninsula's southeast, was one of five large provinces during the Koryŏ dynasty (918-1392)—Yanggwang-do, Kyŏng-sang-do, Jeolla-do, Gyoju-do, and Seohae-do. Kyŏngsang-do is now divided into two administrative districts: Kyŏngsangbuk-do and Kyŏngsangnam-do.
[142] Part of the Sobaek Mountains, which cut across the southern Korean peninsula.
[143] The first and second paragraphs of this 58-page Kim Tonguk Collection were nearly erased. These are

"If you can have a child after praying to heaven, who on earth would be childless?" Minister Paek laughed. "But if you insist, we'll go there together and pray for a child."

Henceforth they performed daily ablutions. Bearing their precious belongings, they ascended to the highest peak of Mount Sobaek, prayed devoutly for a child, and returned home. Lady Paek conceived a child on that very day.

Months passed. One day clouds and mists surrounded Minister Paek's house, filling it with an unusual fragrance. Lady Paek gave birth to a son. Suddenly a fairy came down from heaven, washed the baby with perfume from a jade bottle, and tucked him into bed[144].

"This baby was formerly a hermit officer in heaven. Accused of flirting with a fairy named Sugyŏng in Yoji Pond, he was exiled to the world by the Great Jade Emperor. Heaven has designated this baby to marry a girl named Sugyŏng. You must raise him devoutly and follow the will of heaven." The fairy repeated the request and returned to heaven.

Regaining consciousness, Lady Paek called in the Minister and told him the story. He examined the baby, whose face was as handsome as jade affixed to the front of a crown, his crying sound clean and clear

---

translations of texts that come from the 58-page Kim Tonguk Collection.

[144] The phrase "and tucked him in bed" is borrowed from the 58-page Kim Tonguk Collection because the original phrase was erased.

as a hermit. Minister Paek named his son Sŏn'gun[145].

When Sŏn'gun grew up, he was strong and healthy, adept in everything and deserving of the praise he garnered from everyone. He was fifteen.

"Sŏn'gun must have been a hermit officer in heaven," said the people in the village.

Minister and Lady Paek loved their son dearly.

"Sŏn'gun must find a wife sooner or later, but where to look?" Minister Paek said. He began to search for a daughter-in-law.

* * *

Meantime Sugyŏng was also living in exile, in Ogyŏn-dong, having been accused of flirting with Sŏn'gun in heaven[146]. She heard that Sŏn'gun was looking for a wife, not knowing of his heaven-sent wife because he had been born in this mundane world[147].

"You and I are destined to live in exile in this world and marry. But if you seek someone else, our heavenly tie will have been for naught," she thought.

One day Sugyŏng appeared in a dream to Sŏn'gun.

"How can you propose marriage to other families without remembering me? Have you forgotten we were exiled to this world? The Great Jade Emperor

---

[145] Sŏn'gun (仙君) means a hermit.
[146] Borrowed from the 58-page Kim Tong-uk Collection—the original phrase was erased.
[147] This sentence was completed with material from the 58-page Kim Tong-uk Collection.

sent us here because we flirted with each other at the pond of Yoji. We're destined to marry in this world. Why are you looking for someone else to be your wife? Please wait for me for three years."

She repeated this several times before vanishing into thin air.

Sŏn'gun woke up to find it was a dream—which he vividly remembered. Her face was beautiful enough to cause a flying wild goose drop dead from shame and make the bright moon hide behind clouds and flowers shy[148]. In short, she was as gorgeous as

---

[148] These are three of the four famous old Chinese metaphors for extremely beautiful women: 1) fish underwater; 2) a flying wild goose dropping dead from shame; 3) the bright moon hiding behind the clouds; and 4) flowers feeling shy. Fish and birds were introduced in the text of *Zhuangzi*, one of the two major Daoist classics along with *Laozi* in ancient China.

> *Wang Ni said, "How could I know that? Still, let me try to say something about this. How could I know that what I call 'knowing' is not really 'not-knowing'? How could I know that what I call 'not-knowing' is not really 'knowing'? But now let me take a stab at asking you about it. When people sleep in a damp place, they wake up deathly ill and sore around their waist—but what about eels? If people live in trees, they tremble with fear—but how about monkeys? Of these three, which 'knows' what is the right place to live? People eat the flesh of livestock, deer eat grass, snakes eat centipedes, hawks and eagles eat mice. Of these four, which 'knows' the right thing to eat? Monkeys mate with monkeys, bucks mount does, male fish frolic with female fish, while humans regard Mao Qiang and Lady Li as great*

the bright moon rising from the clouds. Her white teeth shone through her half-opened red lips, her voice rang in his ears, and memories of her jade face glimmered before his eyes.

Sŏn'gun was lovesick. When he took to bed, his parents didn't know what to do.

"There must be some mysterious reason for your illness," said Minister Paek. "Don't hide anything from us. Tell us the truth."

"Some days ago, a jade-face girl appeared in my dream. She said she was a fairy from the Moon Palace and my heaven-sent mate. She told me not to marry anyone but to wait for her for three years. When I think of her beauty, one day feels as long as three years. But I don't know how I can wait for her. Since then, I've been sick to the marrow of my bones."

"When I gave birth to you," said Lady Paek, "a fairy came down from heaven and told me such things. She must be the girl named Sugyŏng. But

---

beauties—but when fish see them they dart into the depths, when birds see them they soar into the skies, when deer see them they bolt away without looking back. Which of these four 'know' what is alluring? From where I stand, the transitions of Humanity and Responsibility and the trails of right and wrong are hopelessly tangled. How can I discern which is right among them?"—From "Equalizing Assessment of Things" in "The Inner Chapters" from *Zhuangzi: The Essential Writings* (2009), translated by Brook Ziporyn and published by Hackett Publishing Company (pp 17-18).

dreams are nothing. You shouldn't care for her. And you shouldn't skip any meals."

"Even if my dream is empty," he replied, "a vow's a vow. I won't eat anything." He lay down and never rose again.

His parents, embarrassed, felt sorry for him. They sought a variety of herbal medicines, which Sŏn'gun ate to no avail.

In Ogyŏn-dong, Sugyŏng knew that Sŏn'gun was sick. Nightly she appeared in his dreams. "How come you're so sick over a humble woman like me? Take this medicine." She showed him three jade bottles. "The first bottle contains the elixir of eternal youth, the second, the elixir of everlasting life, and the third will cure ten thousand diseases. Please take them and wait for me for three years." She vanished.

His illness, however, worsened.

Sugyŏng appeared in his dream again. "Your illness is worsening and your family is growing poorer. So I brought you a pair of golden boy statues and a drawing. You'll get rich if you put the statues on a shelf in your bedroom." She gave him the picture. "This is a portrait of me. Use it as a blanket at night and hang it on a folding screen by day." Then she vanished.

Rising from sleep, he placed the statues in his sleeping room and hung the painting on the folding screen. From time to time he gazed at her portrait, as though it were her.

"There are precious things in the house of Paek Sŏn'gun," said the townspeople.

They flocked to his house and offered gold, silver, and silk fabric as entrance fees. Despite the accumulation of wealth, however, Sŏn'gun showed no sign of recovery.

Sugyŏng reappeared in his dream.

"I'm so embarrassed and sorry for you, because your condition has worsened and you still long for me. I wish your maid servant Maewŏl would serve you in bed to lift your spirits." Then she disappeared.

This, too, was a dream. Sŏn'gun called Maewŏl the next day and made her his concubine. The new therapy alleviated some of his despair, but his love for Sugyŏng outran his feelings for Maewŏl. His yearning for Sugyŏng grew stronger by the day.

Sŏn'gun's loneliness worried Sugyŏng. "If Sŏn'gun dies of lovesickness," she thought, "even our heaven-designated bond will come to naught." She reappeared to him in a dream. "If you want to see me, come to the Kamun Pavilion in Ogyŏn-dong." Then she disappeared.

He woke from his dream, excited, rose from the bed, and rushed to his parents.

"I dreamed last night that she asked me to come to Ogyŏn-dong. I must go there, my illness is serious."

When he bade farewell to them, his parents laughed.

"Boy, you must be crazy."

They sat him down to prevent him from leaving. Sŏn'gun was very upset.

"I'm so sick I have no choice but to disobey you. I'll find her."

Sŏn'gun bade farewell to his parents, who

reluctantly cleared the way for him.

Sugyŏng and Sŏn'gun Tie the Knot

Sŏn'gun felt refreshed. He placed a golden saddle on a white horse and headed for Ogyŏn-dong, searching for it in vain. Unable to calm down, he looked up to heaven and prayed. "Oh! Omniscient god! I pray for you to open the way to Ogyŏn-dong so that I won't miss my chance to marry her."

He galloped deeper into the mountains. Without finding his destination, however, he saw the sun sinking in the west. Ogyŏn-dong seemed far away. It was not until Sŏn'gun hurried deeper into the forest that he came upon the spectacle of steep mountains and deep valleys spreading like a folding screen; a large pond filled with lotus flowers [149]; drooping willow branches dancing in the wind; golden orioles flying high and low; fluttering butterflies lusting after beautiful flowers, teasing the spring; the fragrances of flowers soaking into his clothes. Such a scene did not belong to the human world.

Carried away by the spectacle, Sŏn'gun rode deeper into the forest, where a glorious pavilion towered in the sky, bearing blinds woven with strings of beads. A sign said, *The Kamun Pavilion in Ogyŏn-dong*.

---

[149] Lotus flowers are symbols of enlightenment in Buddhism, because they grow clean and pure in a dirty pond; they are associated with purity, spiritual awakening, and faithfulness.

He strode, enraptured, onto the podium. A young woman rose from her seat. Bashfully, she lowered her slender eyebrows.

"What secular guest steps onto the pavilion?"

"I'm just a humble traveler who enjoys the mountain scenery. I'm sorry to have entered this fairyland without thinking you might fear me. I know I deserve death for this."

"If you want to save your life, you'd better get out of here quickly."

Happy to be spared, he was still embarrassed and feared her warning; also that he would never see her again if he missed this once-in-a-lifetime opportunity. He approached her.

"Don't you recognize me?" he said.

The girl pretended neither to hear nor see him. He shut the door and descended the stone steps. The girl, in a yellow-green jacket and crimson skirt, held a fan inscribed with the design of a white crane leaning against a folding screen.

"Please stop a moment and listen to me," she said.

Pleased, Sŏn'gun turned around.

"How could you be so thoughtless," she said, "after being in the secular world? Even though we're a heaven-sent couple, how can I allow you to enter this place and surrender my chastity on our first encounter?"

She asked him to ascend the podium. He obeyed. She talked, parting her beautiful lips.

"How can you be so thoughtless?" she asked again.

He wanted to rush to her, but he remained calm, taking her jade-like hands.

"Now that we've met, I will have no regrets even if I die straight away," he said[150].

"You said you've been lovesick, which is not proper for a manly man. We came down to the secular world because of our crime in heaven and we're supposed to marry in three years, with a blue bird serving as the old woman go-between, enacting the six proper rituals of wedding[151]. If I surrender my chastity to you now, against the will of heaven, it will be a catastrophe. Please wait three years so that we may enjoy marriage until death separates us."

"When I think of our reunion, one day lasts three years," he said. "I can't count how many days I should wait when you say three years. If you ask me to go home, my life will end tonight or tomorrow morning. Will you be happy if I'm a lonely ghost in heaven? I prostrate myself and pray to you. If you surrender your chastity, it will save my life. Please bend your honor a little, like the pine and the nut

---

[150] The missing words do not interrupt the flow of the text.
[151] In old Korea, a wedding ceremony comprised of six proprieties (*yungnye*; 六禮): 1) a letter and an envelope used for the marriage proposal and acceptance of the proposal by the bride's family; 2) the groom's family's request for information about the bride's hour, date, month, and year of birth for a fortune-teller and the bride's mother's maiden name; 3) notification of any auspicious sign in the fortune-telling to the bride's family; 4) presentation of a wedding gift from the groom's family; 5) selection of an auspicious day for the wedding and informing the bride's family of the date for acceptance; and 6) the groom's greeting the bride in her house.

pine, and save a man poor as a fish caught in a net."

Sŏn'gun's willingness to take his life left Sugyŏng in a dilemma: she could neither take a step forward nor back on the peak of a high mountain. No matter how deeply she thought about this, she could find no solution.

In the middle of the night, the moon shone in the sky. Sŏn'gun slid under the blankets and she followed him and gave herself to him. Sŏn'gun shared a pillow inscribed with the design of a couple of mandarin ducks and fulfilled his long-cherished love. They shared their love with each other, like a couple of mandarin ducks taking a stroll on blue water and common Indian kingfishers gathering on a fused pair of trees. They spent their first night together.

In the morning, Sŏn'gun said, "I'm so happy. From now on I'll never think of the mundane world even if my body is cut by the Yongch'ŏn sword[152] or burned in a red-hot furnace. Now I know this is the real beautiful world. Who would envy high rank and fame?"

"No matter how strong a man's desire, how can you be so shameless? I can't resist you anymore. Now that my body is no longer pure, it's no use for me to pursue learning. I'll descend the mountain to follow you."

---

[152] The Yongch'ŏn sword (龍泉劍), which was said to be the world's most excellent sword, had its origin in a folk song indigenous to Cheju-do. The sword also symbolized masculinity and thus had a sexual connotation, and so it was sung by both men and women.

She readied herself for the marriage procession. She rode on a jade palanquin led by a blue lion. The newly married couple reached the groom's house.

* * *

Sugyŏng prostrated herself to her parents-in-law, who greeted her with propriety. Looking closely at her, Minister and Lady Paek found their daughter-in-law a woman of peerless beauty with snow-white skin and a face pretty as a flower. Her cheeks were like peach blossoms fluttering in a spring breeze. They loved her so much they offered the couple a bridal chamber in the eastern detached house. Their conjugal affection deepened.

Sŏn'gun spent all his time with his wife, never thinking of leaving her even for a second. His parents worried over his neglect of learning but they couldn't scold their only son.

Time passed. Eight years after their marriage, the couple gave birth to a daughter and a son, Ch'unyang and Tongch'un. The family grew richer. Sŏn'gun raised a new building called the Kamun Pavilion in a garden and shared joy with her every day. One day he wrote "Playing Kŏmun'go[153] and Lute, Enjoying Spring in Paradise" and recited it while his wife played *kŏmun'go*. The song was pure and beautiful, even better than traditional Chinese folk songs:

---

[153] *Kŏmun'go* is a Korean musical instrument with six strings—a six-stringed Korean zither.

Two lovers drink wine and exchange poems,
and drink one cup of wine after another.
I watch the jade-like face of my lover get tipsy
in the cozy night.
Next morning, please bring kŏmun'go *if you*
want.

When she finished singing, Sugyŏng was enraptured and lingered under the moon. Seeing her beautiful posture, Sŏn'gun couldn't calm his heart of love.

His parents were pleased with their love and flattered them: "You two must have been a hermit officer and a fairy from heaven in former life."

But one day Minister Paek called Sŏn'gun.

"The state-run examination will be held soon. It's time for you to go to the capital, get out in the world, and gain fame by passing the examination so that you can glorify your parents and bring honor to our family." The Minister pressed his son to take the examination.

Sŏn'gun said, "Our family is one of the wealthiest in the nation, with as many as a thousand slaves. I can enjoy whatever government officials do and satisfy my pleasure. Why should I bother to take the examination?"

Sŏn'gun didn't want to part with his wife, even for a second. Sŏn'gun went to her boudoir to tell her what his father said. He reaffirmed his decision not to take the examination.

Sugyŏng straightened up to say, "It's the duty for a courageous man to rise in the world and gain fame, glorify his parents, and bring honor to his family. If you won't take the examination, afraid of parting with me, how can you distinguish yourself in the world? Not only your parents but other neighbors would believe you renounced this precious opportunity because you are infatuated with me. Think again. Put aside your love for me for two months and go to the capital to win first place in the civil service examination. It will not only bring honor to your parents but make me feel complete happiness. Such joy will be indescribable."

She prepared his travel gear. "If you don't take the examination, I can't live any longer."

She gave him several thousand *nyang* of gold and silver coins and prepared half a dozen servants and an excellent horse with a silver saddle. He reluctantly mounted the horse. It was the middle of March in the Year of Kyŏng'in. Sŏn'gun bade farewell to his parents.

"In my absence please take care of my parents and young children. I'll return as soon as I can after passing the examination. Then we can share our love." He was sad to part with her.

Sugyŏng Wrongfully Accused of Infidelity

No sooner had Sŏn'gun set off on his journey than he looked back at every step to gaze at Sugyŏng standing by the inner gate. He walked no more than thirty *li* from home that day before taking his quarters. He sat down for dinner, but couldn't eat, longing for his wife.

His servant, feeling sorry for him, said, "How can you go on a long journey without eating?"

"I can't eat or drink because I'm so sad." He went to a vacant room, thinking only of her.

Sŏn'gun tossed and turned all night. Her beautiful face glimmered in his eyes and her voice rang in his ears. Around midnight, seeing his servants were asleep, he left his quarters, put on his shoes, and went back home. He jumped over the wall and entered his wife's boudoir.

"What made you return home in the dead of night?" said Sugyŏng, surprised.

"I went down the road all day, but couldn't go more than thirty *li*. I settled in my quarters but couldn't eat or sleep, longing for you. So I came back to see you before going on."

The two talked and enjoyed their time together.

Minister Paek was inspecting the house, worried that a burglar might take advantage of his son's departure. He turned at the wall and entered the eastern detached house, where he heard a male voice in her daughter-in-law's room. He was suspicious, but soon changed his mind.

"Her fidelity is white as a lily-white jade. Why would she meet another man?" he thought, leaning furtively against the window of her room to listen.

Sugyŏng, sensing his presence, said, "I think your father's outside the door. You should hide."

She pretended to comfort Tongch'un, singing a lullaby. "Rock-a-bye baby. Hush-a-bye baby. Your father will return soon after passing the state-run examination, with top honors."

Sugyŏng soon shook her husband awake. "Your father looked all around the doorstep and left, so you must leave quickly. If you return again, unable to forget me, and are found by him, I'll be scolded. Strengthen your heart and set out again. Win first place in the examination and bring honor to our family. Then we can enjoy our time forever." She sent him away.

Sŏn'gun reluctantly returned to his quarters. His servants were still asleep.

The next day he set out on his journey. But he stopped and took up quarters less than fifty *li* away, still unable to overcome his longing for wife. After dinner, he lay down forlornly, feeling sick in his impatience to see her again. Ignoring her warning, he snuck past his sleeping servants and went to her room again. Sugyŏng was surprised almost to death.

"Why can't you forget me and think of your honor and success? I may as well die."

Sŏn'gun pitied his wife after she had consoled him. They had a long talk[154].

---

[154] The following dialogue was introduced in the Kapjin Collection:

Sugyŏng said, "How can you come to me at night without forgetting me. When your precious body falls ill, you'll be at your wit's end. If you really can't forget me, I'll come to your quarters tomorrow." He said, "A young lady is supposed to reside only in a boudoir, so you'll find it hard to go out on the street at night. How could you make such a long journey?"

"Come to think of it, I have a clever scheme." She gave him a picture and said, "This is a portrait of me. When the color fades, it will be a sign that something has happened to me." Thus they were

The Minister was loitering again by the eastern detached house, listening to a man's voice.

"It's really strange!" he thought. "How can a faithful woman meet a man from outside? And how could he enter her room when my house has high walls and more than a thousand servants?" He couldn't resist his curiosity and his fury, but he returned to his room.

Sugyŏng, sensing again her father-in-law's presence on the doorstep, pretended to comfort her baby, singing a lullaby.

"Rock-a-bye baby. Hush-a-bye baby. Now let's go to sleep."

Sugyŏng hid all traces of her husband's presence. Sŏn'gun returned to his quarters, feeling sad.

The next day Minister Paek talked with his wife about this, then called Sugyŏng.

"I've been inspecting my house day and night, fearing that a burglar might take advantage of your husband's absence. The other day I was surprised to hear a man's voice in your room. Last night I heard the same voice in your room. You must tell me what happened."

"It's so boring at night that I talk with Tongch'un and Maewŏl. How could I bring a man in from outside and chat with him?"

Minister Paek was relieved, though suspicious, having heard a man's voice in her room.

He summoned Maewŏl. "Have you recently visited my daughter-in-law's room?"

---

about to part each other.

"I've been too tired lately to visit her."
Feeling more suspicious, he scolded Maewŏl. "During the past few days, I heard a man's voice in Sugyŏng's room at night. I asked her to tell me what happened, but she said, 'I called Maewŏl and talked with her because I was bored.' But you tell me you've never visited her. This is very suspicious. Some goddamned fellow must be having an affair with her. Keep watch on her room and let me know what you learn about him."

Maewŏl monitored Sugyŏng's room day and night, but found nothing strange.

"Since Sŏn'gun married Sugyŏng, he hasn't looked at me for over eight years. Who knew how his indifference broke my heart?" she thought. "I'll feel much better if I slander her."

She stole gold and silver coins from the house, then said to her fellow servants, "I'll give a thousand *nyang* of gold and silver coins to anyone who heeds my request."

Among them was Tolsoe, a sturdy, treacherous, and covetous man, who readily agreed.

"I'll give you all the gold and silver coins," she said, "on condition that you obey my order. It's a fact that before his marriage to Sugyŏng young master Sŏn'gun let me serve him in bed. But after his marriage he never even looked at me. Who would understand my rancor toward her? Day and night I thought of defaming Sugyŏng. Now the time has come, for Sŏn'gun has gone to the capital to take the state-run examination. You must do what I tell you. First, hide by the door to Sugyŏng's room. When I tell my lord what happened, he will surely come here. Pretend to come out of Sugyŏng's room and take flight when you see him approaching. Then he'll believe Sugyŏng was unfaithful, and will interrogate her. Sugyŏng will find it hard to avoid disgrace. Follow my directions without fail."

She went into the Minister's room. "As you directed, I monitored her room for a few days, and when I saw a guy enter it I hid so I could hear what she told him: 'When my husband returns from the capital, we must kill him, then steal treasure from the house and leave.'"

Furious, the Minister drew his sword and went to Sugyŏng's residence. There he saw a sturdy, eight *ch' ŏk*[155]-tall man close the door and run for his life. Unable to suppress his anger, he returned to his room and waited for daybreak.

Minister Paek woke up at the sound of a drum heralding daybreak and the crowing of a rooster in a faraway village. He summoned all the servants and divided them into two flanks, left and right, and harshly questioned them.

"You must know that no one can enter our house because the walls are so high. You must know who entered my daughter-in-law's room. Tell me the truth." Then: "Bring her here!"

His voice was loud enough to shake heaven and earth. Maewŏl rushed into Sugyŏng's room. She yelled at Sugyŏng, stamping her feet.

"What made you fall into such a deep sleep? How

---

[155] One *ch' ŏk* equals approximately 30.3 cm.

could you let your adultery be discovered less than a month after your husband's departure? The minister himself witnessed a guy running from your room and is interrogating us innocent servants. Now he summons you. You must hurry!"

Sugyŏng had barely gone to sleep after spending all night calming Tongch'un. She woke to Maewŏl's merciless scolding, and heard loud voices outside the room. Maewŏl kept pressing her to hurry to her father-in-law. Calming herself, she put on garments and an ornamental jade hairpin. When she emerged from her room, she heard servants whispering.

"For lack of what did our young lady commit adultery in her husband's absence," they said, "and got caught? Why is she so cruel as to let us be flogged?"

Sugyŏng turned pale, astonished.

"What are you talking about? I'm innocent." She rushed to her father-in-law and knelt before him. "It's still dark. Why did you order the servants to bring me here when I've broken no law?"

The Minister angrily scolded her. "When I looked around your quarters some days ago, I heard a man's voice. Suppressing my anger, I asked you what happened. You said, 'I've been bored at night since my husband's departure, so I talked with Maewŏl and Tongch'un.' Maewŏl told me she hasn't visited your room recently. Last night I saw a sturdy, eight *ch' ŏk*-tall fellow close the door of your room and run away. How do you explain that?"

Sugyŏng, crying, found it hard to escape his accusation, despite her excuses.

"You're still making excuses for what I saw with my own eyes. There must be more hideous crimes I haven't witnessed." Minister Paek grew even angrier.

"My father-in-law's order is as solemn as that of the monarch, but I'm as innocent as a lamb. Oh, ghosts of heaven and earth and the sun, the moon, and stars—you all know I'm guiltless! Please clear me of this false charge!" She pounded her chest.

Old trees on the hill dripped, ghosts cried, so did heaven and earth. Everyone wept, except Maewŏl and Tolsoe. Minister Paek grew angrier yet. "I'll find the man you slept with," he said, ordering servants to bind her hands and flog her.

Her hair was wild as a cloud, tears covered her jade-like face, and blood sprouted from the skin ripped and torn by flogging. How could she live? Sugyŏng narrowly regained consciousness.

"Though I'm a daughter-in-law who married without following the six wedding rituals, how can you accuse me of this? You say you saw something that angered you. You won't believe whatever I say. But please examine the facts. Ever since I was born, I've maintained my fidelity as precious as jade in broad daylight, believing that a woman of virtue marries but once [156]. With heaven watching my conduct, how could I commit adultery?"

She wept, pitiful beyond description. Minister Paek only grew angrier.

"A woman in an aristocratic family deserves

---

[156] In the Chosŏn dynasty, a chaste woman was not supposed to serve two husbands.

capital punishment ten thousand times just for having a man from outside visit her. I clearly saw one in your room. How can I regard this as an ordinary affair?" He shouted, "Flog her harder!" Tears flew from her beautiful snow-white face. She barely stayed awake. "I'll tell you the truth. When my husband left for the civil service examination, he couldn't make it more than thirty *li*. Nor could he sleep in his longing for me. So he returned to me. I persuaded him to go back to his quarters. But he returned the next night. I made every effort to make him go back. I apologize for hiding that fact, because I was afraid of your scolding. Perhaps heaven and ghosts are both jealous of us. Things have developed to that stage. I am unjustly accused and punished. How can I explain this situation to you? How can I face my husband again? Heaven and earth know whether I'm guilty or not."

Sugyŏng thought of killing herself but could not go through with it on account of her husband and children. She fainted instead.

Sugyŏng Takes Her Life

Lady Paek, whose family name was Chŏng, wept because she couldn't bear to watch her daughter-in-law in such a horrendous state. She pleaded with her husband for mercy.

"You're not judging prudently. You abuse your daughter-in-law, who is upright and honest as pine and bamboo, on false charges of adultery. I fear you will meet trouble in the future."

She ran from the main floor, dispersed the male servants, and freed Sugyŏng, taking her hand and wailed.

"We foolishly forgot your chastity, and things went bad. Don't complain about false charges. I know how faithful you are. Why don't you go to the detached house and calm yourself down."

"There is a saying—'theft can be pardoned, but burned skin doesn't heal[157].' How can I live when I have been wrongfully accused? I'd rather die and forget everything."

Lady Paek tried every possible means to persuade Sugyŏng to think otherwise, but she wouldn't listen. Sugyŏng removed her jade hairpin from her hair and looked heavenward.

"Oh, bright and brilliant heaven, be my witness. I wish you would distinguish justice from injustice! If I committed adultery, let this jade hairpin penetrate my chest now! If not, let it be stuck in a stone step in the garden of the main floor until my husband returns!"

She threw the hairpin into the air, where it fluttered in the wind before flying into one of the stone steps and lodged there. Sugyŏng lost consciousness again.

Minister Paek was so sorry that he would have pulled out his eyes if he could. But it was too late.

---

[157] The Kapjin Collection mentions another version of the text: "There is a saying that 'theft can be pardoned, but prostitution cannot be forgiven.'"

The servants, whispering, were at once amazed and ashamed.
Minister Paek rushed to her, grabbing her sleeves. "Please forget the talk of an old man in his dotage. Just calm down!" He made every effort to console her.
Sugyŏng, once pure as snow and ice, was now embittered. She thought she wouldn't be sad if she died ten thousand times, nor happy to be reborn a thousand times.
"This false accusation will not vanish as long as I live." She vowed to take her life.
"False charges of improper relations between men and women are common. Why be so sad?" Minister Paek tried in every way to convince her to calm down, to return to her boudoir.
Sugyŏng wept, grasping her mother-in-law's hands. "If I am to be known to the world as an unfaithful woman, that knowledge won't disappear for more than a thousand years. How can I be free of shame?" Her jade-like face was wet with pearly tears.
Lady Paek scolded her husband. "You've turned her fidelity, clean as ice and snow, overnight into unfaithfulness. How can she not feel bitter? When Sŏn'gun hears the news of her death, he'll follow her to heaven. You'd better take measures to stop her lest there be some tragedy." She blamed her husband over and again. "My lord! Act now."
Sugyŏng saw her daughter Ch'unyang and son Tongch'un, aged seven and three. Ch'unyang clutched Sugyŏng's skirts.
"Mom! Mom! Don't die now," Ch'unyang cried.

"You must live with us. When you die, how can I live? What will happen to Tongch'un? When dad comes back, you can tell him the truth and give vent to your feelings. Tongch'un is crying for milk. Why don't you go inside and feed him. Whom should we rely on without you?"

Ch'unyang led her mother into the room. Sugyŏng breastfed the baby, with Ch'unyang seated beside her. She pondered the situation. "How can I forget my time in heaven and Yoji, while living in this filthy world?" she asked herself.

She thought of her husband and children. She felt fire rising in her liver to burn all her other internal organs. Her snow-white face turned dark as inky clouds, her weeping voice produced a bowl-breaking sound. Quietly flowing tears soaked the collars of her dress. She took out all her pretty rainbow-colored dresses and stroked Ch'unyang's hair.

"Alas! Ch'unyang! I must die today, because heaven hates me. When your father returns, tell him exactly what happened so that he can console the woman who died embittered." She cried bitterly for a while and said again "This fan with the design of a white crane is a precious jewel of the world. It produces warm wind when it's cold and cool wind when it's hot. Please give it to Tongch'un when he grows up. Those seven treasures[158] and silk dresses will be of great value. Wear them when you grow up. After I leave this world, give Tongch'un water when he's thirsty, feed him when he's hungry, and soothe

---

[158] Gold, silver, lapis, crystal, coral, agate, and pearl.

him when he cries. Oh, my Ch'unyang, I wish you'd get along without looking askance at him. Have pity, Ch'unyang! What will become of poor Tongch'un. My heart is heavy. Oh, my Ch'unyang. Whom shall you two rely on now?" Sugyŏng wept buckets.

Ch'unyang cried at the top of her voice. "Mom! Mom! Why are you so sad? When you die, whom shall we rely on? I'll follow you and die, too. Poor Tongch'un! You were born in this world but may find it hard to grow up healthy. How vexed I am!"

Mother and daughter embraced each other, sobbing, until Ch'unyang fell asleep, holding her mother's skirts. Sugyŏng stroked her sleeping daughter.

"I've considered it many times. But how can I face anyone in this world? I'll clear these charges by going to the next world." She petted Tongch'un, thinking, "I die now with regret that I won't watch you grow up."

She bit her finger and wrote a letter with her blood. After posting it on a wall, she stroked Ch'unyang and Tongch'un, who were already asleep. "Have pity, Ch'unyang! Poor Tongch'un! Whom shall you rely on now?"

Sugyŏng put on a silk dress and rested her head on a pillow embroidered with a pair of mandarin ducks. She took in her delicate hands a dagger ornamented with jade, and hesitated, debating whether to take her life. She wept again.

"I'm dying, leaving my children in swaddling clothes, without seeing my husband who is far away. I fear I will not be a benevolent ghost."

She raised the dagger high and stabbed herself in the chest. The bright daylight darkened and the sound of thunder shook the whole world.

Startled, Ch'unyang and Tongch'un woke up to find their mother with a dagger in her chest, covered with blood, dead. Ch'unyang tried to pull the dagger out to kill herself. It didn't budge. The children sobbed, clutching her corpse, burying their faces in her.

"Mom! Mom! What happened to you? Take Tongch'un and me where you're going!" Their crying was loud enough to be heard from a great distance.

Minister and Lady Paek and the servants rushed to the scene. They found Sugyŏng with a dagger in her chest, and tried to pull it from her. But the dagger of the revengeful ghost did not move. What to do? Everyone was at a loss. Tongch'un tried to suckle his mother's breast, crying in hunger, not knowing she was dead.

Ch'unyang consoled him. "Mom fell asleep. You can suckle when she wakes up." Then she wailed. "How can we live together now that mom is dead? Have pity on us!"

She held her mother, rubbing her cheek against her. "Mom! Mom! Day has dawned bright. Wake up! The sun has risen above the horizon. Tongch'un is crying for milk. He won't listen to me even when I give him a piggyback or carry him in my arms. He eats nothing though I gave him boiled rice and water. He only wants milk." Ch'unyang took Tongch'un in her arms, saying, "We'd better follow mom now to the underworld."

No one at the scene could look at them directly. Not only mountains and rivers but grass and plants and animals were sad. Light from the sun and moon faded, mountains and rivers remained melancholy. Even those with iron hearts could not resist weeping.

Day finally broke. They found on the wall a letter written in blood:

> *Alas, since coming into the world charged with a crime in heaven, I have been tied to my love in wedlock. We didn't forget each other even for a minute. My husband didn't covet rank or fame but thought only of me. So I persuaded him to take the civil service examination, but perhaps ghosts were jealous of us or the creator deity*[159] *hated our happiness. Pure as white jade, I was wrongly accused of adultery. Who will heed my feelings? My heart aches as I hold this dagger and watch my children sleep. I don't regret dying now, but my children—who will they rely on? I'm bewildered, thinking of their future. And my husband, who left a month ago, is a thousand* li *away. I feel so sorry for him. How can his heart be comforted? Our vows of*

---

[159] The creator deity here is different from the Christian God. But it is interesting to note that such a concept existed in the East. Buddhism rejects the existence of a creator deity, refuses to endorse many views on creation, asserts that questions about the origin of the world will not end suffering, but states that Mystic Law governs the universe, the world, and all matter.

eternal love came to nothing. My love! My love! I wish you would come back as soon as possible, dispose of my dead body, clarify my innocence, and console my soul, which could not relieve its deep sorrow. I have much more to say but my resentful heart precipitates my departure from the world.

Three days after her death, Minister and Lady Paek thought: "Our daughter-in-law is dead. When our son returns and sees a dagger in her chest, he will think she died because of our slander. Surely he will try to kill himself. We must dispose of her body before he arrives."

They entered Sugyŏng's room and tried to shroud the corpse. But it didn't budge. The Minister and his wife and all the servants were stunned. They didn't know what to do.

Sŏn'gun Passes the Civil Service Examination

Sŏn'gun arrived in the capital, where scholars were flocking to the civil service examination site. After a few days, he entered the testing ground carrying his examination kit, and saw the topic for the essay on the signboard: *The Voices of Children's Songs on Peaceful Streets*[160].

---

[160] The translation follows the essay topic introduced in the Kim Kwang-sun Collection: "The Voices of Children's Songs on the Public Streets" (Kanggu mun tongyo; 康衢聞童謠), which means "the nation is peaceful and

After contemplating the topic for a while, Sŏn'gun dashed off his essay with one stroke of his brush, submitted it to the administrator before the other contestants, and left. The Emperor[161] read Sŏn'gun's essay and gave it high praise. "This could not have been written by a human. Such glittering, jade-like sentences! And the calligraphy is as vigorous as the movements of a flying dragon. This scholar surely possesses marvelous talent."

The Emperor searched for the examinee's name: *Paek Sŏn'gun in Andong, Kyŏngsang-do*. He chose Sŏn'gun as the first-place winner and made him a scholar in the National Academy of Royal Documents. Sŏn'gun expressed his gratitude to the Emperor and went to work at the Academy. He wrote two letters—one to his parents, the other to his wife. His servant traveled day and night to deliver them to his parents. The Minister opened the letter:

I offer my greetings to you and ask how you are. Thanks to your devotion, I am getting along quite well. Heaven blessed me to become the first-place winner of the civil service examination and a scholar of the National

---

prosperous."

[161] The proper expression here should have been "the king" (from the hereafter) instead of "the Emperor," because Korea did not adopt an imperial system until the reign of Kojong, the penultimate monarch of the late Chosŏn dynasty.

> *Academy of Royal Documents. I will return home on the fifteenth of this month. I hope you will prepare a celebration.*

Weeping, Lady Paek delivered the other letter to Ch'unyang. "This is a letter from your father to your mother. Keep it in your bowl." Lady Paek sobbed.

Ch'unyang, holding Tongch'un in her arms, returned to her mother's boudoir. Weeping, she shook the dead body, and removed the cloth covering her mother's face. With the letter in one hand, Ch'unyang rubbed her face against her mother's cheeks, and wept.

"Mother, wake up. Father sent you a letter. Wake up. Father's coming home after winning the civil service examination, becoming a scholar at the National Academy of Royal Documents." Ch'unyang covered her mother's face with the letter. "Tongch'un cries every day for breast milk. You loved reading so much. Why don't you read the letter? I am sorry I can't read it aloud to your soul because I don't know how to read." Then she said to her grandmother, "If you read it to the spirit of the dead, my mother's soul will be impressed."

Lady Paek entered the funeral parlor reluctantly and read the letter tearfully:

> *I send you a letter of regards with deep affection. Because our love is as grand huge as mountains a thousand* li *apart, I cannot see you even if I wished. I always think of you, though I try not to. Meanwhile I have recently discovered that*

the color of your portrait has faded. I wonder if you contracted a fatal disease. So I can't sleep under the lantern in my quarters. Thanks to your devotion, I won first place in the civil service examination and am a scholar at the National Academy of Royal Documents. I hope this is good news for you. I'll return on the fifteenth day of the month. Please take care of your precious body until we meet again.

Lady Paek cried out, "Ah, Ch'unyang! I pity you and Tongch'un! How will you live without your mother?" Ch'unyang and Tongch'un embraced their dead mother and rolled on the floor, weeping. No one dared to look at such a sad spectacle.

Lady Paek said to the Minister, "In the letter to his wife, Sŏn'gun expressed yearning for her and related the news of his success on the civil service examination. He said he was sick with worry that she might had fallen ill. When he comes home and sees her dead body, he will surely follow her into the next world. What can we do?"

"After worrying about this day and night, I have a good idea. Don't worry." He summoned his servants, and said, "When my son returns and sees the corpse, he'll try to take his life. You take every measure to prevent this disaster."

An old servant said, "A long time ago, I served your son during his visit to a scholar-cum-*chinsa*[162]

---

[162] *Chinsa* derives from the state-run civil service examination. Those who passed the primary level were

named Yim. When a crowd gathered, a young girl whose face was gorgeous as the sun and the moon emerged from the silk curtains and immediately went back inside. Sŏn'gun said, 'She's the paragon of beauty in the whole world.' He asked who she was. When he heard she was the daughter of Yim, he praised her dearly, enamored of her. I suggest you take her as your-daughter-in-law. Coincidently, Yim lives in a region your son will pass on his way back. Your son can hold a wedding ceremony before he gets home. Since he's young, he might forget his old love when he indulges in a new bride. Why don't you hurry to offer Yim's family a wooden wild goose[163] and proceed with the wedding rite?"

The Minister liked this suggestion.

"That sounds good. Yim is my old friend. He'll listen to me. Besides, my son has become a noble figure. Yim will accept this marriage proposal." He rushed to Yim's house.

Chinsa Yim greeted Minister Paek with delight. "What brings you to this humble house?"

"A long time ago, my son met a girl named Sugyŏng and married her. They loved each other dearly and never parted, even for a moment.

---

called either literary degree-holders (*saengwon*) or classics degree-holders (*chinsa*), which qualified them for higher level (*taegwa*) degrees.

[163] In a traditional Korean wedding, the bridegroom's family offered a wooden wild goose to the bride's parents. Wild geese were regarded as auspicious birds that symbolized a married couple happily growing old together.

Perplexed, I sent my son to the capital to take the civil service examination. Fortunately, he won first place and became a scholar at the National Academy of Royal Documents. He sent word that he would soon return. But owing to family misfortune or bad luck, Sugyŏng died a few days ago. As they say, good always comes with bad. When he returns and sees her dead body, he will probably follow her to the next world. To prevent such a disaster, I'm searching for a new wife. Then I heard you have a beautiful daughter. Now I shamelessly wish to propose a wedding to your family. What do you think? My son is still young, and he will forget his old love when he meets a new perfect mate—your daughter. I hope you'll accept my proposal. If your virtuous decision saves my son from death, it will mean great joy and glory for both of our families."

"Last year," Yim replied, "on the fifteenth of July, I saw your son playing *kŏmun'go* and reciting poems with his wife in the Kamun Pavilion. It was as if Wŏlgung Hang'a offered precious peaches to the Great Jade Emperor. Your daughter-in-law was like the full moon in autumn while my daughter is no more than a half-moon shrouded in a dark cloud. He won't forget his beautiful wife. If and when things fall apart after I accept this marriage, what will become of my poor daughter? That would be regrettable."

Minister Paek, however, did not relent, and Yim eventually accepted the offer: "It will be my joy to have your son as my son-in-law."

"Sŏn'gun will pass your house on the fifteenth. We

can hold the wedding then."

Minister Paek sent wedding presents to Yim's house and waited for his son's return.

* * *

Sŏn'gun was on his way home, wearing an indigo jacket and holding a white jade scepter, with a green parasol shielding him from the sun. The procession went on for ten *li*, followed by a group of young *kisaeng*[164]. Pipers played *A Song of Peace* to the accompaniment of the three major stringed instruments[165] as Sŏn'gun rode a white horse with a golden saddle, and people from other regions rushed to watch the spectacle and praise him.

When he arrived at a provincial office, the provincial governor held a welcome party. Sŏn'gun entered the gate with dignity, a royal paper flower[166] affixed to his hat, and a jade belt around his waist. The governor praised him. "You really look like a strong hermit."

Sŏn'gun was so tired from the journey that he

---

[164] *Kisaeng*, similar to courtesans, refer to women trained to entertain male customers with conversation, dancing, and singing, as well as writing and reciting poems.

[165] The three stringed instruments refer to *kŏmun'go*, *kayagŭm*, and *hyangbip'a* in the Silla Kingdom, as opposed to their four-stringed counterpart in the Tang dynasty. *Hyangbip'a* had five strings, though the name of its inventor is not known.

[166] The king bestowed this flower upon winners of the state examination for civil and military service.

dozed off. Half asleep, he saw his wife open the door to the bedroom and enter with blood spilled over her body. She sat by him, weeping.

"Born with bad luck in this world, I couldn't stay any longer, and now I'm in the next world. The other day, my mother-in-law read your letter to my departed soul, so I know you won the civil service examination, became a scholar at the National Academy of Royal Documents, and are coming home. How could I not be happy to hear this news even in death? You're returning as a man of honor. I've come here because I was so happy at your returning. But nothing is as desperate as the fact that I can no longer see you in this world. Alas, my husband, what will become of Ch'unyang and Tongch'un? Hurry home to comfort them. They're grieving over their mother's death, crying for their father. Grown gaunt, I walked this road step by step, falling forward and backward. You must touch my chest." She heaved a deep sigh and wept.

Pleased to see her, Sŏn'gun took her hands and touched her body, only to find a dagger stuck in her chest. Stunned, he asked her what happened.

She said in a choked voice, "When you left home for the civil service examination, you came back twice to see me. Ghosts must have hated us. Maewŏl accused me of infidelity, with whopping lies which my father-in-law believed. I couldn't find a way to rid myself of this slander, so I took my life." She heard a rooster crowing in a distant village. "I'm a dead spirit, so I have to get before dawn." And then she vanished into thin air.

When Sŏn'gun woke, he realized it was just a dream. He sat up straight, recalling his terrible nightmare. He heard the sound of a drum heralding three o'clock, dawn, and the crowing of a rooster. He called his servant and pressed homeward day and night.

Minister Paek had arrived at the house of Yim, accompanied by his servants and equipped with wine and food—a party awaiting his son. The Minister saw him stop spurring his white horse from his golden saddle. He nervously went in and out of the hall several times, then took the hands of his son. "I cannot hide my joy because you won the civil service examination and became a scholar at the National Academy of Royal Documents."

He offered his son a cup of wine. Sŏn'gun held the cup with both hands and drank, pleasing the Minister, who said, "You work for the National Academy of Royal Documents, your face is as gracious as Tu Mokchi's, and you're handsome. I think an excellent gentleman like you cannot be satisfied with only one wife, and as I sought far and wide for a wise woman for you, I heard the daughter of Yim is a rare beauty. Thus I made a formal proposal of marriage to him, and we decided to hold the wedding ceremony today. How do you like my idea?" The Minister tried to persuade his son to accept the proposal.

"On my way home," said Sŏn'gun, "my wife appeared to me in a dream covered in blood. She sat down beside me, touched her chest, saying little. Perhaps something happened to her? I still cherish my vow to her. I won't make a decision until I talk to her."

Sŏn'gun spurred his horse, trying to pass Yim's house. But the Minister caught him by the hand and tried to soothe him.

"You're not behaving like an aristocrat. Marriage is the greatest event in human affairs. It's a son's duty to have a wedding in observance of the six proper rituals, following the will of his parents to glorify his family. Why are you so stubborn about this? If you fail to marry her right now, it will ruin her future. It also goes against the proper conduct of a man of virtue."

But Sŏn'gun urged his horse forward without a word.

A servant advised Sŏn'gun. "Aren't you supposed to follow your parents' will? Yim's family will be offended when you pass by his house. You should think this over."

Sŏn'gun chided his servant and galloped on. Helpless, the Minister followed his son. When they arrived at their house, he seized his son by the arm and spoke, weeping.

"You've come home with a great success. Let me tell you something. After you left for the capital to take the civil service examination, I heard a man's voice in your wife's room. Curious, I asked her who she was talking with. She lied to me, saying she was chatting with Maewŏl. I grew more suspicious, I warned her as her father-in-law, and for various reasons she took her life. Nothing on earth is more terrible than this."

Turning pale, astonished and afraid, Sŏn'gun cried. "Is it proper now, after deceiving me, to persuade me to marry the daughter of Yim? Has she really died?"

Sŏn'gun Puts Maewŏl and Tolsoe to Death

Sŏn'gun galloped his horse like a drunk or crazy man, rushing to the inner gate of his house. The sorrowful cry from the eastern detached house was heard even outside the gate. With tears gushing like spring water, Sŏn'gun entered the gate and saw a jade hairpin stuck in the stone steps. He plucked it out and wailed again.

"You, cold-hearted hairpin, greet me. Why does my warm-hearted wife fail to come greet me?" Wailing loudly, he entered the eastern detached house.

Ch'unyang carried Tongch'un on her back, crying bead-like tears, and shook her mother's body in the funeral parlor, crying all the while. "Mom, please wake up! Papa has passed the civil service examination and come home." From her back Tongch'un saw Sŏn'gun and cried. Ch'unyang clutched her father and fell down weeping.

"Pa, mom has died. Tongch'un clings to mom and cries for milk every day."

Sŏn'gun embraced his children, wailing with them. Eventually he lost consciousness holding his dead wife in his arms. When he regained consciousness, his children shook him and rubbed their cheeks against his. He removed the cloth covering his wife and saw a sword stuck in her chest. He turned to his parents. "How pitiless you are! You haven't even drawn the dagger out!" He rubbed his cheek against hers. "My darling! I've come back. Please wake up! Wake up!"

When he pulled the dagger from her, three blue birds flew out. One bird sat on his shoulder, crying. "*Hamyŏnmok, hamyŏnmok!* (Disgraceful, disgraceful!)" Another sat on Ch'unyang's shoulder, crying, "*Soijo, soijo!* (Pure little child, pure little child!)" The last one sat on Tongch'un's shoulder, crying, "*Yugamsim, yugamsim!* (Regrettable, regrettable!)"

Listening carefully until the birds flew away, Sŏn'gun interpreted their words. "*Hamyŏnmok*" means, "Wrongly accused of adultery, how can I face my husband?" "*Soijo*" means, "Dear Ch'unyang, please take good care of Tongch'un." "*Yugamsim*" means, "Dear Tongch'un, I can't close my eyes because of my regret over deserting you at such a young age." The three birds symbolize three souls and seven spirits[167] of Sŏn'gun. The crying of the birds symbolizes her farewell address to Sŏn'gun from her deathbed.

Then the corpse began to rot. Sŏn'gun held her in his arms, wailing.

"My darling! I don't want to see Ch'unyang and Tongch'un cry for their mother. Poor soul! Please breastfeed Tongch'un. You were so healthy. Where

---

[167] Three souls and seven spirits are what constitute the human body: three spiritual and three physical constituents. In Buddhism and Daoism, there are different ways to interpret the seven spirits, including the seven holes in the body or seven types of greed.

did you go after deserting me? I'm so bitter! Take me with you. I hate this. I hated my journey to the civil service examination. What good was it to pass? Even when I wore a golden dress or ate delicious food, I missed you so much that each moment seemed to last three years. Now that you're dead, I won't see you again even after a thousand years. How can I take care of my children? How can I live without you?" He held on to her. "I have no reason to live. I'll die and meet you in the afterlife.

He looked at his children. "Ch'unyang! How will you live now? Oh, you poor little thing. Tongch'un. I don't know what will become of you."

He wailed at the top of his lungs and again lost consciousness.

Ch'unyang and Tongch'un cried. "Poor dad! If you die of grief, how can we live alone?"

Ch'unyang cried, holding Tongch'un. She fed and soothed him with water.

"Don't cry. When dad dies, we can't live in this world. Let's follow him and rely on the dead spirits of our parents."

She gave one hand to Sŏn'gun's and held Tongch'un with the other. Mountains and streams, plants and grass and all the animals seemed to wail altogether.

They entered the room. He touched Tongch'un's head. Ch'unyang sat beside him. She said, "Tongch'un wants us to feed him when he's hungry and give him water when he's thirsty. We have to carry him on our back." Sŏn'gun lost consciousness again.

Ch'unyang said, "Pa, aren't you hungry or thirsty? Mom poured wine made from various flowers into this jade bottle to serve you when you return. Please drink it. Then I'll tell you mom's dying words. Don't be so sad. Take pity on Tongch'un and me. Have some wine." She filled Sŏn'gun's jade cup. "What's the use of drinking wine and living in this world?" he said. "But I will do it for your devotion and to follow your mom's dying wish."

He was about to drink it when tears dropped into his cup and spilled over. Ch'unyang wept.

"Mom said before she died, 'Alas! I don't care whether I die or not. But how can I shut my eyes in the afterlife when I was wrongly accused of adultery? Worse, I must die without seeing your father, who is a thousand *li* away. I made for him a full-dress attire and a belt to wear when he returns from winning the civil service examination. Now I've finished embroidering one wing of the white crane. Tell him to wear them as if he saw me.'" Ch'unyang took out the attire and belt, and said, "Why don't you look at the style and design of the dress?"

He saw the dazzling silk robe with blue silk innings shining in five colors. First, he felt his whole world collapsing. When he looked at them again, he felt his chest tighten. Then he was dumbfounded. Now that he finally saw them, he felt his eyes dulling, his liver and bowels meandering slower and slower until they had decomposed.

"How can I live after witnessing such a wretched scene?"

***

Ten days passed. Sŏn'gun thought, "I let Maewŏl offer me bed service. After I met Sugyŏng, though, I treated her coldly. She must have held grudge and slandered her."

He ordered the servants to arrest Maewŏl and bring her to him. Then he forced her to kneel, saying, "You must tell me the truth."

"I've done nothing wrong."

Sŏn'gun, angry, ordered the servants to flog her until she confessed. She couldn't endure the pain, and so, reluctantly, told him what happened.

"Who visited my wife's room?"

"Tolsoe."

Tolsoe was standing among the servants when Sŏn'gun yelled, "Arrest him and tie his hands."

With a triangular club in his hand, Sŏn'gun ordered Tolsoe to tell him the truth.

Tolsoe cried. "I coveted gold coins, Maewŏl tempted me to commit this crime. I committed a dreadful crime without thinking about the consequences. I deserve to be executed."

Sŏn'gun ordered his servants to beat him to death, took his sword out, approached Maewŏl.

"How can I let such a filthy woman like you live in this world?"

He stabbed her to death in the stomach.

He went to his father and said, "How could you trust the words of such a treacherous bitch so that my wife, who was pure as white jade, would die alone?"

The Minister couldn't speak. Sŏn'gun prepared the funeral, wrote a eulogy, and arranged his gear. Sugyŏng, disheveled, entered Sŏn'gun's room that night, covered with blood. "Alas, you distinguished good from evil, clearing me of a false charge. And since you killed Maewŏl, I have no regrets even after death. But I can't see you again, I'm a lonely spirit in the afterlife who deserted Ch'unyang and Tongch'un. I still hold a grudge against heaven. Alas, my husband. Please bind my corpse with six-year-old sweet flags and drop me in the pond of Ogyŏn-dong, burying me neither in a new nor an old grave. Much later, I will be able to see you and Ch'unyang and Tongch'un. Please listen to my request without thinking it strange. If you don't fulfill my request, I won't be able to fulfill my wishes. Then our children, too, will likely meet an unfortunate destiny. Please comply with my last wish."

She vanished into thin air. When Sŏn'gun regained consciousness, he knew it was a dream.

Sŏn'gun rushed to his parents to tell them his dream. He decided to hold a funeral after cleaning and shrouding the corpse. But the body did not come unstuck from the floor. The whole family was at a loss what to do. Sŏn'gun pondered.

"She was wrongly accused, died in disgrace, and became a lonely spirit in the next world, leaving Ch'unyang and Tongch'un behind. How could her soul feel comfortable?"

He tried in every way to console her spirit. But the corpse wouldn't budge. It wasn't until Sŏn'gun, deep in sorrow, dressed Ch'unyang and Tongch'un in mourning clothes and rode them on a horse before a bier that the coffin began to move swiftly forward as if flying.

Sugyŏng and Sŏn'gun Ascend to Heaven

When the pall-bearers arrived at the pond of Ogyŏn-dong, Sŏn'gun saw water overflowing and the beam of the waters reaching the sky. He sighed, not knowing what to do. Then it became dark everywhere, and the mountains and rivers lost their colors. The waters drained, turning the pond into bare land. Looking closer, he saw a stone coffin. The people placed the dead body inside and buried it. Then lightening and thunder and five-colored clouds surrounded Ogyŏn-dong as the pond filled with water. Sŏn'gun turned toward the water and read a funeral ode:

> *On a certain day of a certain month in a certain year[168], I, Paek Sŏn'gun, a royal scholar, dare to report this to the spirit of my beloved. We met thanks to the ties of past, present and future, loved like a pair of mandarin ducks or common Indian kingfishers, and pledged to be united as husband and wife for better or worse. But maybe some were jealous of our love or ghosts made mischief. During the several months of our parting, you innocently became*

---

[168] This marks the typical beginning of a funeral oration in Korean society old and new.

a lonely spirit wandering the nether world without committing a crime. How could I not be sad? But now that you have returned to the nether world, who should I rely on to raise Ch'unyang and Tongch'un? I had planned to bury your body on the knoll in front of my house so I could visit you often. But if I put your corpse in the water, how can I see you in the afterlife? The mundane world and the afterlife are two different things, but human affection will remain the same anywhere. So I ardently wish to meet you again. I offer you pure wine. Please take it.

Sŏn'gun fell flat on his face, crying. It was as if the plants and grass and all the animals grew sad and mountains and rivers fell down. Then the boiling waters were separated with a roaring. Sugyŏng, wearing yellow-green jackets and crimson skirts and decorated with seven treasures, rode on the back of a blue lion emerging from the water.

Sŏn'gun and the mourners, greatly astounded, said altogether, "How can she come back alive when she died ten days ago and was just a dead ghost in the water?"

Sŏn'gun held onto Sugyŏng. Uncovering her white teeth half between her red gums, she said, "Don't be afraid of anything. Just follow me to meet your parents and then go up to heaven." She returned home riding on the blue lion.

Seeing Sugyŏng return with their son, Minister and Lady Paek rushed out of the room, gasping.

"Where have you been?" They were bewildered.

Sugyŏng approached her in-laws and prostrated herself.

"I was destined to suffer tragedy because of my crime in heaven. Everything boils down to the heavenly mandate. So you don't have to grieve anymore. The Great Jade Emperor has ordered us to return to heaven. We can't resist the order, so we'll go up to heaven together."

Minister and Lady Paek wept. Sugyŏng offered them a fan designed with a white crane, a bottle of spore wine, and a bottle of medicinal wine.

"This fan, the most famous treasure under heaven, will produce warm wind when it's cold. You can live for a hundred years if you keep this fan and take this medicine when you don't feel well." She continued, "When you die, you're supposed to go to the Lotus Flower Palace in Buddha land. No need to be afraid. Hermit officers of heaven frequent the palace for business, so we will gladly visit you there."

Sugyŏng looked at Sŏn'gun. "It's time for us to go to heaven. Let's offer parting words to our parents." Sŏn'gun shed tears, thinking of the love between parents and child. He went to his parents, prostrated himself to them, and offered his parting words.

"Your humble son must part with you because our relations in this world are ending. Please live in peace."

Sugyŏng offered her farewell greetings then called a pair of blue lions. Sŏn'gun and Sugyŏng held Tongch'un and Ch'unyang, respectively, in their arms, surrounded by five clouds. The two lions rode up to heaven on the rainbow.

Minister and Lady Paek lived absent-mindedly for a while, unable to hide their grief. As time went by, though, their grief gradually subsided [169]. They distributed all their property to their poor neighbors and idled away their later years. When they turned one hundred, they died on the same day at the same time.

People heard wailing from Churyŏng Peak on Mount Sobaek—the prelude to the appearance of mist. Clouds and mists surrounded the Minister's house for three days[170]. After the clouds and mists disappeared, the neighbors found everything they needed for the funeral, including boards for the coffins in which they buried the couple on Churyŏng Peak.

From then on people said, "Hermits used to enjoy their time on Churyŏng Peak."

---

[169] Part of the text is missing.
[170] Part of the text is missing.

About Translators

Sohn Tae-soo, who is teaching translation at Sungkyunkwan University in Seoul, is a Korean-to-English translator, specializing in the sector of the Korean studies and academic papers, among others. Formerly a reporter of The Korea Herald, he received a doctorate degree in the interdisciplinary study of English literature and English translation of old Korean literature from the same university. His main interests are English translation of Korean literature and philosophical texts as well as academic journals. His translations include: *21 Icons of Korean Culture* (2009); *Korean Education: Educational Thought, Systems and Content* (2018); and *Ahn Jung-geun's Vision for Peace* (2018).

Won-Chung Kim is a professor of English Literature at Sungkyunkwan University in Seoul, Korea, where he teaches contemporary American poetry, ecological literature, and translation. He has published articles on American and Korean poets in *ISLE, Foreign Literature Studies*, and *CLCweb*. *East Asian Ecocriticisms: A Critical Reader*, which he co-edited with Simon Estok, was published in 2013 at Palgrave Macmillan. His book, *Food Ecology*, was published in 2018 by Geobook. He is the recipient of Freeman Fellowship, Daesan Translation Grant, and KLTI Translation Grant. He has translated twelve books of Korean poetry including *Because of Rain: Korean Zen Poems*, *Cracking the Shell: Three Korean Ecopoets*, and Seungja Choi's *Phone Bells Keep Ringing for Me* (2021 National Translation Award Long List) into English. He has also translated John Muir's *My First Summer in the Sierra* and H. D. Thoreau's *Natural History Essays* into Korean.

Christopher Merrill has published seven collections of poetry, including *Watch Fire*, for which he received the Lavan Younger Poets Award from the Academy of American Poets; many edited volumes and translations; and six books of nonfiction, among them, *Only the Nails Remain: Scenes from the Balkan Wars*, *Things of the Hidden God: Journey to the Holy Mountain*, *The Tree of the Doves: Ceremony, Expedition, War*, and *Self-Portrait with Dogwood*. His writings have been translated into nearly forty languages; his journalism appears widely; his honors include a Chevalier des Arts et des Lettres from the French government, numerous translation awards, and fellowships from the John Simon Guggenheim Memorial and Ingram Merrill Foundations. As director of the International Writing Program at the University of Iowa since 2000, Merrill has conducted cultural diplomacy missions to more than fifty countries. He served on the U.S. National Commission for UNESCO from 2011-2018, and in April 2012 President Barack Obama appointed him to the National Council on the Humanities.

www.ingramcontent.com/pod-product-compliance
Lightning Source LLC
Chambersburg PA
CBHW032020230426
43671CB00005B/151